Dear Susan,

May your future be blessed
with His riches!

Sincerely, Jason Jensen

12/13/13

BREAK IT

5 Rules
Every Investor
Must Break

Jason Jenkins

Published 2012 by Lamp Publishing

To book Jason Jenkins for a speaking engagement, visit
www.breakit-book.com

Printed in the United States of America

ISBN-10: 0-9849286-0-X
ISBN-13: 978-0-9849286-0-6

Contents

Acknowledgements

This book could not have happened without so many people who have impacted my life, which has helped shape this book. First and foremost my thanks goes to my wonderful family that surrounds me and encourages me on a daily basis. To Jennifer, my amazing wife, who is patient, loving, and supportive, to whom this book is dedicated. She allows me to accomplish so much and encourages me to follow my heart. To my children, Hunter and Julia. Hunter is a son that every father prays to have. His compassion, intelligence, and insight at such a young age inspires me to be a better father, husband, and friend. Julia brings a smile to my face every morning. Her heart is full of life, which makes me stop and be thankful for what I have and to give 100 percent. There could be nothing more precious than her beautiful brown eyes and gorgeous smile that lights up my day.

To my parents, who have sacrificed their lives for me and my brother. I believe it takes time for children to see and understand the sacrifices that parents go through. You have led by example of what true love means, and I am eternally grateful. To my brother Brad, you are as solid as they come. I am grateful to have you in my life and the counsel you have provided. You are truly the best brother that one could ask for. To the rest of my family who has been supportive and loving, I appreciate all that has been done for me.

After my family is my friends, who have taught me about life in ways only a friend can. As you walk through life, you find out through trials the ones who love you and support you.

To Casey McGee and Todd Emblem, who since college have stood beside me though thick and thin. Craig Van Hulzen, you have been not only a great friend but the best counsel in the investment industry. Nathan Knecht, you define what a friend is suppose to be and set the standard. Dr. Senyo Adjibolosoo has been the most amazing mentor that anyone could ask for. Your life has forever influenced mine and I would not be the person I am today if you had not been a part of it. To Mike Amodeo and Ed Hidalgo, whose friendship has encouraged me to be all that the Lord has for my life.

Finally, this book was not able to come together without the help of many others. Michael Riendeau, whose research and support along the way has been incredible. This book would not have had its in-depth perspectives if it was not for you and your hard work. To Kaitlin Nadal, who took my thoughts and words and help put them together. You are a first-class editor, and all I can say is thank you!!! To my Aunt Janet, for the book cover concept and the illustration in the book. I wish I had your talents. To Claude Prettyman, you are a talented designer and you brought this book cover from concept to a great final product. To Isaac Bitar, thank you for the picture on the cover and your work on the graphs for the book. To Pastor Bob Botsford, for your message that the Lord used to inspire Rule 5 in this book. Thank you for being such an authentic and passionate man for Christ.

To all these people, I am deeply grateful. THANK YOU!!!

—Jason Jenkins

Introduction

The Monkey and His Bananas

In February of 2007 I found myself in Ghana, Africa in a small town called Akatsi. Dr. Senyo Adjibolosoo, my former MBA professor at Point Loma Nazarene University, was in the beginning stages of building a school that would provide education from kindergarten to college, and I was there to help him. Through this and subsequent trips to Africa with Senyo, I have been blessed to be immersed in Africa's rich culture.

Since the beginning of time, people have found wisdom in nature and through past experiences in storytelling. A narrative tradition, deeply rooted in the African culture, carries this wisdom forward to teach each next generation. Stories that have been passed down for hundreds of years help illustrate some of life's most basic, but crucial, life lessons.

On this particular trip, Senyo shared several different stories with me after dinner in the hot, muggy African evenings. There is one that I would like to pass along to you as we venture into this book of investment wisdom. This story comes from a small island fishing village called Dùdú in the Keta Lagoon, based on a telling by Togbui Peni Blemewu Adjibolosoo.

It was a warm and humid morning among the many trees of this tropical rainforest. It was, in fact, the most beautiful rainforest that one could imagine. This rainforest blanketed with tall trees created a canopy to all the wildlife that called it home. As the sun began to rise, the awakening of Mother Nature pushed its way through the forest. In this rainforest lived a tribe of monkeys high up in the trees. One of the monkeys had known these trees since he had been born, and he was raised in this exact area. This monkey enjoyed his life, for he had all the food he desired and the company of friends and family surrounded him. Some would say the monkey was living the good life.

But there was something special about this monkey. He was a talented, skillful, and bright monkey. Besides his skills, he possessed a strong desire to seek out new frontiers for himself and his family. The problem was these desires never got past his daydreaming. Every day he said to himself that there must be something more beyond the land that he knew. But his daily routine was set. Every morning, he went to do what he had done every day of his life—get up and eat and provide food for his family. Like most monkeys, the most precious thing to him was his bananas. Now the bananas in this rainforest were not just ordinary bananas. This monkey's tribe considered them special bananas. Indeed, the elders of his monkey tribe declared that God himself watered the soil in which those bananas grew.

So one day, as was his routine, the monkey went over to the tree to grab several bananas to eat. As he was lying back eating his bananas, he also began to dream of what he wanted for his future. As these thoughts were beginning to wrestle in his mind, out of the trees came two monkeys from a different region. Messy and disoriented, they quickly asked, "Can we eat from this tree, as we have traveled from a distant land and we are hungry?"

The monkey hesitated for a moment. These were his precious, God-given bananas. After thinking about it he finally replied, "Yes." These two monkeys did not know that they had just asked for something so precious. The travelers quickly began to fill up on bananas, without seeming to taste them.

The monkey who called this little area home was confused. He was excited to share this wonderful experience that he treasured on a daily basis. Why weren't they rejoicing and exclaiming over such divine sustenance?

"Did you enjoy the bananas?" the monkey asked.

"Yes, thank you," one traveler replied, a puzzled look on his face.

"Were they not the most delectable bananas you have ever tasted?" the monkey asked.

"They were good," said the other traveler. "But I have certainly had better."

The first traveler nodded in agreement. The monkey was astounded. Could his treasured banana grove hold nothing but average bananas?

As they sat around eating the bananas, the two monkeys from the other region told him they were just passing through to reach a forest of plenty for themselves and their families, with the most plentiful and tasty bananas in all the land.

"This journey requires certain skills that we do not possess, and we have been traveling in search for someone who has great scouting skills, is courageous, and is not afraid of the uncertain," they told him. "We cannot find this place without someone with these skills."

As the monkey was hearing this, his heart began to pound, his eyes opened with excitement, and a grin came across his face. The monkey gulped down his last bite of banana and said, "That is me! I have all of what you just said and more. I desire to have more, so much more than what is being offered here. As much as I love my home and these bananas, I believe there is more for my future as well. If you would let me join you on this venture, I would be so grateful to you."

So the other two monkeys quickly discussed this matter and replied, "Yes, we would like for you to join us on this quest for greater fortunes. So let's get going now, for we cannot waste any more time."

In hearing this news, the monkey jumped up and started grabbing a bunch of bananas for the journey ahead. As he did, the other two monkeys asked in wonderment, "What are you doing?"

He replied, "I am taking with me the bananas that I love and cherish for the journey ahead."

One of the other monkeys replied sternly, "You cannot bring those! If you truly want the greater fortunes that you say you so desire, then you must leave those bananas behind. We must move quickly, and those bananas are going to slow us down. We will find more along the way."

The monkey was shocked, as shocked as if he had just lost a family member. He asked himself, "How could they ask such a thing? How could I leave behind what I have come to know as my life and truth? This is all that I know."

As these thoughts were running through his mind, the other monkeys declared, "Well, if you cannot make this sacrifice, then you were never meant to reach the goals you desire. As talented as you are, you lack what you need, which is a willingness to sacrifice what you know in order to achieve a higher level of success. Sometimes what you know today can hold you back from a brighter tomorrow."

One last time, they told the monkey to drop the bananas and come with them. As he stood there, his eyes welled up with tears, for he knew in his heart that he could not let go of the one thing he loved the most, the bananas. So the two monkeys slowly turned and walked into the forest, never to be seen again.

As the days and years passed, the monkey often wondered whether his visitors ever reached the land that they had spoken of. As the monkey grew in age, one day news came that one of his worst nightmares had come true. The monkeys who had invited him to come along had indeed found the land they dreamed about. When this news came to the monkey, his wonderment of years turned into a deep sense of regret. He then began to ask himself the "what if" questions. What would life have been like for me and my family if I had left these bananas? Would it have been what I dreamed about? As he thought, he finally realized what had been holding him back from leaving with the other monkeys. It was the fact that he could not let go of his old habits. He had formed a wall of ignorance, pride, and fear that did not allow him to see beyond the rainforest around him.

I share this story to ask you to leave your bananas behind as you read this book. What are your precious bananas? As you read this book, you will bring your personal investing experience and knowledge, and these can be the bananas that may get in the way of you being open to changes to your investment future. Come into this book with an open mind, so that you can possibly unlock what might be a better path for your financial future.

This book is designed to help give you the framework to make sound investment decisions that meet your long-term goals. This book doesn't address everything. It will not train you on how to time the market, to spot undervalued stocks, or to know when to get in and out of certain bonds positions. This book is written to address critical rules that need to be broken to help put you on a path of financial security. I believe this book is going to speak to your intuition and your gut, to make you have an aha moment where you say to yourself: I knew it. I also believe it will challenge you to rethink your current assumptions about investing and change certain aspects of your portfolio or verify what you are doing already.

There are always new rules to be broken. As the brilliant bestselling author William J. Bernstein said in his book *The Four Pillars of Investing* (New York: McGraw Hill, 2002, xiv), "Personal finance, like most important aspects of life, is a never-ending quest. The competent investor never stops learning." Take your time in this book, and never give up on seeking knowledge, especially in such a crucial area of your life.

1.

Rule 1: You Can't Control Your Investment Outcome

"An investor without investment objectives is like a traveler without a destination."
Ralph Seger

One of my best friends from college, Todd, is a pilot for Southwest Airlines. Several years ago, as he was going through the pre-screening process to become a pilot, we had a lengthy conversation about the robust safety training and procedures that pilots endure in order to operate planes at Southwest. I had always assumed it was not easy to become a commercial airline pilot, but hearing about the hours of flight simulations, examinations, and medical screenings firsthand made the stringent requirements more real.

Several weeks later, I was traveling from San Diego to Sacramento on Southwest and, as I was taking my seat, the conversation that I had with Todd began to replay itself. I have never been a nervous flyer, but since that conversation, my confidence and peace of mind when it comes to flying has grown even more, because I know how many logbook entries, flight condition checks, equipment inspections, and maintenance procedures go into even a single flight from San Diego to Sacramento.

One thing Todd said, something I've since shared over and over, struck a deep chord with me: A great pilot "knows and understands his or her limitations and capabilities at all times."

A great pilot knows what he or she *cannot control* while flying. This is critical for dealing with the situations that can arise unexpectedly while in flight—from a thunderstorm, to an engine going out, to black ice on the wings or a passenger out of control. Todd said that even though pilots do not know if any of these things will happen on a flight, they must be trained and ready to respond to ensure the safety of all crew and passengers on board the flight if they do.

In my industry, as in aviation, one of the most important keys to successful investing is knowing what you *can and cannot control as an investor*. You may have been told that there is very little you control about your investment outcome. You may feel that once you invest, you're at the mercy of the whims of the market. You may think that investing is little more than a giant crapshoot.

Well, that is not quite accurate. There is in fact a sizable chunk of your investing decisions that you can control. In many ways, you actually can control your investment outcome. At the very least, you can tip the scales in your favor. These are the first two critical questions that I ask my clients to think about:

1. What *Can* I Control In My Investments?
2. What Can I *Not* Control In My Investments?

Below is a chart to help you see what can be controlled when it comes to your investments and what is out of your hands. As an investor, you need to understand each one of these decisions and the links between them. For, as you read this, you have already made decisions as to what you believe you can control and what you believe you cannot control. But what you may not be aware of is the exact impact—or more accurately, the consequences—associated with each one.

What I *Cannot* Control	What I *Can* Control
• Movement in the stock market • Shifts in political conditions • Shifts in legal situations • The state of the economy • Interest rates and inflation • Credit risk • Companies' stock performances • My emotions	• Do-it-yourself investing • Hiring an investment advisor • What type of advisor I hire: commission-based or fee-based • My investment philosophy: passive or active • Rebalancing my portfolio • My reactions to my emotions • Asset allocation: risk to my portfolio • Withdrawal rate from my portfolio

Your initial response here might be, "I already know that! If this is how this book starts out, then I'm not going to get anything substantial out of it." Whoa, hang in there for a second! I want you to ask yourself another question:

How good am I at actually IMPLEMENTING these things that I already know in my investments on a daily basis?

Maybe this question makes you uncomfortable. Or maybe you do implement these things when making investment decisions. If so, here's a follow-up question:

How do I know that I am following the correct, or the most optimal, plan to achieving my financial goals?

Let's assume that you are on the right path to achieving your financial goals. If so, I have one more question for you. In fact, this is the most difficult question that investors face on a daily basis:

How good am I at staying DISCIPLINED and sticking to my long-term financial strategy?

If this last question tripped you up, don't worry, because you're not alone. Most investors are not disciplined because they have not been given the tools and emotional skills needed to achieve this discipline. They can start strong, but quickly they can begin to drift into a territory that they were never meant to be in.

If you are reading this and saying to yourself that you are

extremely good at staying disciplined and not getting emotional when markets move up and down, then congratulations! You belong to a select group that consists of very few individuals. For the rest of you, I will address this issue of discipline head-on in this book and equip you with the skills you need to become a disciplined investor.

If you do belong to that first select group of investors, someone in your life has probably given you the right emotional framework to approach the markets and the emotional discipline to stay the course to meet your financial objectives. Whoever that person is in your life—whether it's a financial advisor, parent, mentor, friend, or other family member—I want you to call him or her right now and say "Thank you!" for positively impacting not only your life, but also the generations to follow you. If you are confident about your long-term financial plan and the discipline required to achieve it, this book will be a confirmation of your beliefs.

The Investment Planning Process

I have sat down over the years with hundreds of investors, and the first thing they usually want to do is dive headfirst into the investment process by deciding which funds to buy for their portfolios. While this is understandable, it's not the proper first step to establishing an investment plan.

You need to undergo a process of financial analysis that will help shape your investment decisions and ultimately produce a written investment plan. But before getting there, you need to begin with an honest assessment of several crucial factors that affect all investors:

1. **Where are you today?**
2. **Where do you want to be in the future?**
3. **How will you get there?**
4. **What do I value?**

You do not start by looking *outward* to what investments strategies you will implement, or what types of mutual funds or stocks you will buy. Rather, you begin with an *introspective* look at your goals, resources, and needs so that you can build a plan with a purpose.

As Bill Bachrach said in his book *Values-Based Financial Planning: The Art of Creating and Inspiring Financial Strategy*, "In the grand scheme of things, money's not that important. It's significant only to the extent that it allows you to enjoy what is important to you. And not worrying about your finances is critical to having a life that excites you, nurtures those you love, and fulfills your highest aspirations."[1]

If you want to accomplish great things in your financial life, you must have a sound financial strategy that is designed to help do so.

An honest assessment of these crucial factors applies not just to individual investors, by the way—it also applies to the world's largest pension plans, endowments, and insurance companies. In fact, an entire industry of consulting firms exists whose sole function is to help guide large institutional investors through this very process, because they understand the value of starting from the right foundation.

---

1. Bill Bachrach, *Values-Based Financial Planning: The Art of Creating and Inspiring Financial Strategy*, Aim High Publishing, 2006).

The importance of establishing a sound financial road map from the beginning cannot be overstated. In my experience, however, the proper time is not given to this by most investors. Many approach investing thinking that they cannot control their investments, making planning unnecessary, or that good plans are centered on the sale of a product. I disagree: Setting a foundation to any successful plan is about starting with answers to these fundamental questions, through which you, the investor, clearly understand what truly is in your control and what isn't. I will discuss this more later in the book, when we delve into how emotions impact our financial decisions. The academic world calls this "behavioral finance."

> "The greatest enemy of a good plan is the dream of a perfect plan."
> —Karl von Clausewitz, Prussian General

Permit me for a moment to state something that should be obvious: As an investor, you are looking to make the smartest possible decisions about your money. Whether you are a wealthy, high-net-worth individual with millions of dollars to invest, or a middle-class family with more modest assets, you must have a comprehensive investment plan to make those decisions.

There is a process to establishing an investment plan that I lay out in the "Take Action" section. The formula is: *Gather, Reflect, Plan, Implement, and Revisit.* I present this formula in an outline format for you to follow and take action on.

Creating Your Investment Plan

When it comes to investing, one of the most powerful tools that does not get the attention it deserves—or in my opinion, demands—is a written investment plan. If you are working with a financial advisor, he or she should be providing what I am about to go over with you in this section.

Large pension plans and endowments use such plans, known as investment policy statements (IPS). A written investment plan is the end result of performing a financial analysis to help answer the three investment assessment questions. In answering these questions, you'll cover such areas as your specific investment goals, your time horizon, your personal comfort with investment risk, and the investment strategies that you will follow.

By putting all of this in writing, you are taking an important step toward assuming control of your financial future. You will be in a position to have clarity and focus on the long-term goals you are targeting as part of your investment strategy.

Investment policy statements should encompass the following six key areas:

- Establishing long-term investment values, needs, and objectives (or goals)
- Establishing an investment time horizon
- Determining rate-of-return objective
- Determining proper asset allocation
- Determining an acceptable level of risk that is commensurate with your return objectives
- Establishing an investment methodology

I would like to touch first on the importance of long-term investment values, needs, and objectives. Every investor makes choices to invest for the achievement of financial objectives that are tied to his or her own value system. Focusing on values helps you move into a deeper level of engagement with your overall investment goals because of their connection to your fundamental, pure, and personal emotional identification.

When you begin to think about values, try to focus on the power you feel that comes from these emotions: accomplishments, achievement, balance, independence, pride, providing for family, making a difference, spiritual attainment, inner peace, and self-worth.[2]

> "Money, like values, means different things to different people."
> —Bill Bachrach

Long-term financial success truly means different things to different people. For some, success is funding college educations for their children, while for others it is maintaining a comfortable lifestyle in retirement. For this reason, it is critical that you uncover your financial values and objectives early in the process of creating your investment plan.

One of the leading authorities on this subject is Bill Bachrach, whom I noted earlier. Bachrach trains financial advisors worldwide about how to address the issue of values and goals with their clients, so I wanted to pass along a few nuggets of information from him to help guide you through this very important step.

---

2. Bill Bachrach, *Values-Based Financial Planning: The Art of Creating and Inspiring Financial Strategy* (Aim High Publications, 2000).

Bachrach recommends you (and your spouse) work through the following series of questions:

1. **What is important about money to you?**
2. **What does financial success look like to you?**
3. **What does financial failure look like to you?**
4. **What do you want for your children? Your parents? Other family members?**
5. **What impact do you want to have in your community?**
6. **When you think about your money, what specific concerns, needs, or feelings come to mind?**[3]

As you wrestle with these important questions, you may find it difficult to establish goals that you are willing to work toward consistently, especially if you and your spouse are not in total agreement.

You need to make sure that your plan has room to be flexible as well, because things change, and so do our values. For example, one day my former MBA professor Dr. Senyo Adjibolosoo approached me with a proposition. He wanted to establish a school in Ghana, Africa, and he offered me the opportunity to assist him. I've since traveled there three times and arranged my budget to continue my support. If you'd have told me several years ago that I would be doing this, I'm not sure how I might have reacted! Now investing in the school is a big part of my life, and my family's life as well.

There are other contingencies to plan for as well. Family members get sick; dear people pass away. Remember, without

---

3. Ibid.

having an end game in mind, you easily can be distracted from sticking to your investment plan. For investors, the beginning of this end game is establishing investment values, goals, and objectives.

You also need to consider whether you possess the skill sets and knowledge required to create your investment plan yourself, or if you should work with an investment advisor. Here are several questions to help you determine this:

1. **How involved do I want to be in the investing process?**
2. **Who else do I want to be involved in investment and financial planning?**
3. **How qualified am I to make sure the plan is properly constructed?**
4. **Do I have the time to constantly ensure my plan is on target?**

The answers to these questions can help you quickly shape your strategy to determine the proper next steps. For example, maybe you realize that you need to hire a professional to help construct a financial plan. A significant part of your financial success will be your ability to stay focused on your goals and stick to your plan. Some investors are in a position where they have the time, training, and temperament to handle investing matters themselves. These are do-it-yourselfers, much like the guy who does minor home or car repairs himself rather than call a handyman or go to the repair shop. I would say, however, that the long-term consequences of making mistakes in your investment plan will likely be much more severe than a botched home or car repair.

Conversely, the majority of investors find themselves lacking the skills, training, time, and tools needed to implement and maintain an investment plan themselves for any reasonable period of time. This is why many hire an advisor to help them. Also, many investors have a lot more money than time on their hands and prefer to delegate the responsibility of financial and investment planning to an advisor. I will discuss this in more detail in the Take Action chapter, to help you understand your options when it comes to seeking investment counsel.

Embracing Risk

Risk is a loaded word. Risk constantly surrounds us, whether it's the risk of getting in an automobile accident every time you step into a car or the risk of injuring yourself by playing a pickup basketball or softball game with your buddies.

So what was your first reaction when you read the phrase above, "Embracing Risk"? I hope you had mixed emotions. Embracing something usually evokes positive, warm, and inviting feelings. When it comes to risk, however, most people want to run the other direction (though a few daredevils prefer to run right at it).

But no matter what you do with your money, there will always be a degree of risk involved—even if you just stuff it in your mattress, you risk losing purchasing power through inevitable inflation. Everyone wants to run from risk, but you are going to lose money if you just hold it. What you must do is understand the different types of risk associated with the financial decisions you make as you continue the process of taking control of your investment portfolio.

You can't run from the fact that there is a relationship between the amount of risk you take with your money and the rate of return you can expect to receive. Stocks do post dividends on their earnings, and bonds do post interest, but these income streams are high-

Your financial future hinges on your understanding of risk. You have to recognize and acknowledge the various types of risk inherent in the investment world, and you have to be realistic about the amount of risk you, your spouse, and your family are comfortable taking.

ly variable and never guaranteed in the future. It is in this uncertainty that the importance of asset allocation arises. As you will see in Chapter 3, the proportion of stocks, bonds, commodities, and REITs in which you invest matters. We all know that no one can forecast the future perfectly, but we can understand that there are different types of risk inside asset classes, so we need to understand the types and see what we can control and can't control.

An investment plan is not complete without an understanding and intelligent assessment of risk. We need to put our arms around this little four-letter word. Investors who fail to understand and assess risk inevitably fall victim to the emotions of hope, fear, and greed—and the result is almost always an overreaction that adversely affects long-term investment performance and returns.

Types of Investment Risk

Risk in the financial world comes in all kinds of shapes and sizes, but there are four primary types of risk that you will face as an investor:

- *Market Risk (or Systematic Risk)*
- *Diversification Risk (or Non-Systematic Risk)*
- *Inflationary Risk*
- *Objective or Goal Risk*

Market Risk is systematic in nature. Interest rates, recession, wars all represent sources of systematic risk, because of the effect they have on the entire market. The best way to think about this is to take a look at recent history. In 2008, you could not hide from the fact that almost every asset class lost value in the harsh reality of the period of time called the "Great Recession." The takeaway for you as an investor is understanding what, under extreme circumstances, a wave of systematic risk could do to your portfolio. There is always this risk. Sometimes you can see certain issues coming, but then there are the ones you do not see, the "black swan" events that send markets unexpectedly tumbling. Examples of a black swan would be the tsunami in Japan, September 11, 2001, or Enron imploding.

Diversification Risk, on the other hand, is non-systematic in nature. It is specific to the risk involved in investing in the stock of a single company, a single commodity, or a single type of currency. Think if you had owned a majority of shares in Washington Mutual during the financial crisis. Or, on the other side, if you would have owned Apple shares over the last eight years. A bull market, for example, cannot help the stock of a company chalking up huge losses. So if you have a portfolio with just a stock position, you are increasing your non-systematic risk in your investment life. By choosing a well-rounded and diversified group of asset classes, this at the very least ensures that your investment goals are not tied to one single stock or group of stocks. This can be true in fixed income as well. If you own just a couple of corporate bonds, government bonds, or municipal bonds, you still are creating a higher non-systematic risk, which can increase the potential volatility in your overall portfolio.

This aspect of managing non-systematic risk is one that you control, and it will be the most important decision you make for your investment portfolio. Where and how you invest your assets is at the marching orders of just one person, ultimately, and that is *you*. Whether you manage your portfolio yourself or hire an advisor, you need to ensure your assets are allocated well to give you the highest probability for success.

Inflationary Risk affects every portfolio and must be accounted for. If the rate of return on your investment portfolio is not keeping up with rising prices (or inflation), you're rowing against the current, and there is no way to get ahead. Imagine a portfolio made up of bonds, CDs, and cash. The investor might feel he or she is mitigating the risks of an unpredictable stock market by sticking with such conservative investments, but the risk of losing purchasing power increases in such an investor's portfolio.

For example, consider that the value of $1 million today will fall to around $440,000 in twenty years, even at a 4 percent inflation rate. Inflation must be factored into your investment plan, and this makes understanding the cyclical markets within the greater secular markets increasingly important.

Objective or Goal Risk is the last, but certainly not the least important, risk that I've listed. In fact, it may be the most important type of risk for investors to understand. This is simply the risk of not having well-defined and achievable investment goals, or having the wrong or unrealistic goals. I have stressed this already in this chapter, but it deserves to be mentioned again to bring the importance to it. This could be one of the biggest mistakes that I see investors make: *They set impractical rates of return to achieve their goals.* This behavior often triggers something that I call *"unnecessary risk."* This is when an investor does not need to take on the potential market risk in order to achieve his or her goals. This idea simply underscores the need for all investors, no matter where you are in life, to have a plan. I know this information is not new or groundbreaking, but sometimes in life the most practical things are the ones that lead to success or failure. It has surprised me over the years how many investors simply do not have a plan. It would be silly to build a skyscraper without a blueprint, so why do that to your future?

I cannot stress enough the importance of understanding these risk factors as you and your financial planner assess your financial goals and set a strategy to achieve them.

What Investment Risk Looks Like

If you Google the words "risk associated with investing," you will discover many different definitions of investment risk. But I believe one of my clients summed it up best when he said to me, "Jason, to me, risk is not having enough money to last for my entire lifetime and maintain my independence from my immediate family."

For many people, this is the ultimate definition of what risk looks like. This definition actually lines up with that of pension funds that view risk through the lens of meeting the obligations to their pension benefactors, beside the part of moving in with their kids. Academics tend to define risk as the volatility of price or return over a specified period of time. Volatility can be measured daily, weekly, monthly, or annually, and in many different ways. It is high volatility that causes the big swings in price movements and market fluctuations, and low volatility that produces more stable and consistent prices and fewer market swings.

As investors seek to achieve the highest possible returns on their investments, there will be periods of loss in their portfolios. The best way to address this issue is to have a broadly diversified, index-fund-based portfolio, which is addressed in detail in Chapter 2.

Trying to escape the realities of risk and return is not possible, but proper asset allocation can help minimize large swings in portfolio values, and possibly the frequency of losses during certain time frames. But there will be times when the portfolio is down in overall value. The key to long-term investing success is choosing an asset allocation strategy composed of the right portfolio mix for your needs and paying attention to certain measurements inside your portfolio. Understanding how to read risk begins to give you some control over risk, so that if another bear market comes along (and it will!), you will be better prepared, so that panic does not set in to such an extreme and you ultimately get sucked into the emotional rollercoaster many investors do that produces only sub-par long-term investment returns.

Volatility: "Please, NO!"

To help you understand volatility, you must come to learn what standard deviation and beta mean to your portfolio. This section may get technical, but push through or reread this to make sure that you gain an understanding of this important information. To keep it simple: Greater volatility means greater risk to the pricing of an asset. There are two basic sorts of investing volatility: historical volatility and implied volatility. Historical volatility is determined by measuring the fluctuations of a given stock based on its past performances. Implied volatility reflects predicted fluctuations, determined through the prices of options related to a given stock. The percentage in which implied volatility is expressed indicates the likelihood that a stock price will rise or fall within one *standard deviation* move in the next year.

Standard Deviation

From an investment standpoint, standard deviation (or SD) shows how much variation or dispersion there is from the average or mean (or expected value). The standard deviation is expressed as the Greek symbol σ (sigma).

A lower standard deviation value indicates that the data points along a bell curve, or normal distribution, tend to be close together, with less room for variation, whereas a higher standard deviation tells you the data points reach out wider, with more variation. An easy way to remember this is that a lower SD will give you less stress but also probably lower returns, while a higher SD can provide greater potential upside but also potentially larger movements to the downside, and thus more stress. So if you were comparing different portfolios to invest and you were presented past historical returns, you would want to see the SD next to each portfolio to understand the risk taken to achieve those returns. For example, see figure 1.1. In this example, there are two portfolios: (A) & (B). If you were just shown the returns, you would probably want portfolio (A) with the higher return, but when you look at portfolio (B), it is clear there is high value to the investor even though the return is 1 percent less. The data you want to examine is the SD, portfolio (A) took on twice the amount of risk compared to portfolio (B). This is taking SD and applying it to your investment portfolio.

Portfolio	Return %	Standard Deviation
A	8.5%	12%
B	7.5%	6%

Figure 1.1 Standard deviation in two sample portfolios

To understand how implied volatility can be useful, consider the example in figure 1.2. We are going to assume in this case that there is normal distribution (as opposed to lognormal distribution, another method of measurement), which gives equal chance for prices to occur either above or below the mean, which in this example is shown as $50.

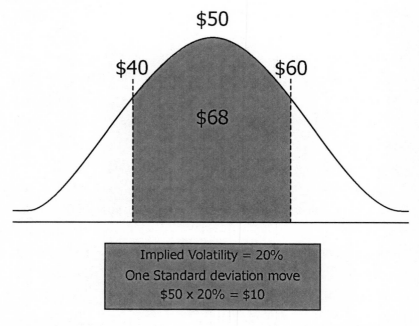

Figure 1.2   Impact of cost on distribution of market returns

Assume you have purchased a certain stock that trades near the current price of $50 and rarely makes an extreme move. The implied volatility is 20 percent, which statistically falls within one standard deviation. A one standard deviation move would be $10:

One standard deviation move: $50 x 20% = $10

Using this information, we can plot the standard deviation chart, which reflects a normal expected price range of between $40 and $60, or in other words, $50 minus and plus $10. At a standard deviation of two, the stock would trade between $30 and $70 ($50 minus and plus $20), and at a standard deviation of three, it would trade between $20 and $80 ($50 minus and plus $30). To give some context, a second standard deviation would be a year like 2008.

The above example is stating a very simple case and does not represent by any means the stock market or a particular asset class. Asset classes have their associated benchmarks, which provide an accurate representation of the standard deviation. The range of volatility in an asset class can and will vary considerably.

Knowing the average standard deviation gives investors a rough idea of the relationship between the historic risk and expected return of an investment. This is why you will see riskier asset classes (such as U.S. small-cap stocks) that have a higher potential return, but also higher risk, with a high standard deviation.

Beta

The second piece of information to analyze is the beta. Beta is the measure of an asset's correlation to the market as a whole. Beta is most commonly measured against the S&P 500. How a beta works can be seen in figure 1.3. A beta of 1 indicates an asset will go up as well as down to the same extent that the market does. A stock with a beta at .70 moves 30 percent less, either up or down. An asset with a beta of zero moves completely independent of the market, and an asset with a negative beta moves up when the market moves down, and vice versa. If a beta of a given portfolio is 1.2, then the portfolio is theoretically 20 percent more volatile than the market. Beta accounts for both the direction and the extent of a given asset's momentum relative to the market. These values are ranked in the following table.

Investment	Beta
S&P 500	1.0
Portfolio A	1.2
Portfolio B	.70

Figure 1.3   Beta inside your portfolio

Both beta and standard deviation provide quantifiable information to help you make investment decisions. Having this information allows you to examine a portfolio mix over a period of time to help you in understanding potential outcomes for a selected portfolio. The fact is, by understanding the amount of risk inherent in a given investment option, you will be better equipped to make decisions that lead to long-term portfolio success. In figure 1.4, you can see all this information coming together to empower you, the investor. Portfolio A is simply not bringing enough value when you compare it to portfolio B. Again, if you are working an investment professional, he or she should be able to provide this information to you on your current portfolio or recommended portfolio.

Portfolio	Return %	Standard Deviation	Beta
A	8.5%	12%	1.2
B	7.5%	6%	.6

Figure 1.4   Putting the standard deviation & beta together[4]

---

4. Ronald Cordes, Brian O'Toole and Richard Steiny, *The Art of Investing & Portfolio Management: A Proven 6-Step Process to Meet Your Financial Goals* (New York: McGraw Hill, 2008).

Lower Volatility = Peace of Mind

So what is the bottom line of all this discussion of risk, standard deviation, and beta? Simply, lower volatility will bring greater peace of mind. When volatility enters a portfolio, it can result in lower returns, so reducing volatility helps move the compounded returns higher over time. It is a matter of what you keep at the end of the day, not what you make. Anyone can make one or two major wins on investments and have ten losers that put them in the hole. I think we saw this in action through the recession in 2008, where people were making a ton of money in real estate and leveraging themselves, only to ultimately lose it all. Maybe you were one of them. Yes, we have to take risks to make money, but wealth in the long run is not created by taking bigger and bigger risks. Some of you may argue this, but time value of money in my opinion is what wins. In taking a big risk, one must be willing to lose it all and have it not affect their financial future inside their portfolio. Again, I'm not talking about business risk or personal risk. I am talking about our risk inside of your portfolio. This is how we see lower portfolio price volatility actually increase portfolio return over time. There is no way to remove volatility, but understanding its impact on your personal goals is possible.

Lower volatility is a true benefit to the investor because it actually can help enhance your overall investment returns over a period of time. As a result, you can build more wealth by managing volatility through proper asset allocation and rebalancing.

Refer to figure 1.5 for an illustration of how the variability of annual returns (or volatility) reduces a portfolio's value over time. Look at the differences between the simple average returns, which are all the same, and the true compounded returns, which are different and affect the actual ending portfolio values. You cannot argue with numbers. Compare Case B to Case F. The compounded return for B is 4.997 percent and for F is 2.361 percent. The lower volatility in Case B contributed to greater returns over time, even if its initial returns were relatively low. Negative returns severely diminish your overall compounded returns.

While most people realize inherently that they need to reduce the volatility in their portfolios, many do not know what it truly takes to get back to where they started when a portfolio takes a loss. For every percentage point in investment capital you lose, it takes more than that to recover it and get back to the breakeven point. The figure 1.6 demonstrates this clearly. If you lose 10 percent in your portfolio, you will need to get an 11 percent return to get back to where you started. Now, I don't want to scare you into thinking, "What if my portfolio was to lose 50 percent?" But I want to help you understand the true cost of volatility.

Dispersion & Negative Numbers

	CASE A	CASE B	CASE C	CASE D	CASE E	CASE F
Year 1	5.0%	4.0%	9.0%	15.0%	25.0%	30.0%
Year 2	5.0%	5.0%	5.0%	-10.0%	-15.0%	-25.0%
Year 3	5.0%	6.0%	1.0%	10.0%	5.0%	10.0%

Simple Average Return
5.000% 5.000% 5.000% 5.000% 5.000% 5.000%

Compounded Return
5.000% 4.997% 4.949% 4.419% 3.714% 2.361%

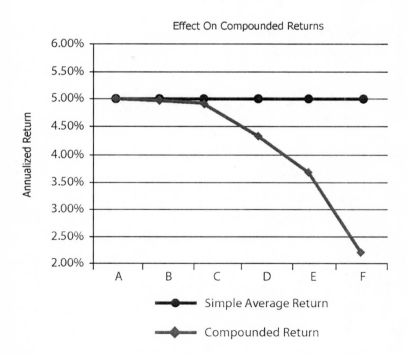

Figure 1.5   Impact of volatility and negative numbers
As presented by Crestmont Research (www.CrestmontResearch.com)

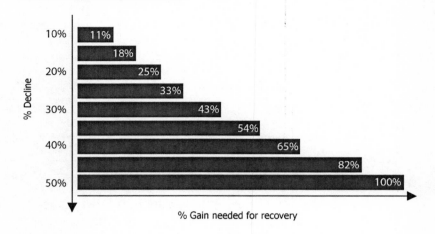

Figure 1.6 The mathematical catch-up game
Information provided by Genworth Financial Wealth Management, Inc.

> *"There are two rules of investing. The first rule is don't lose.*
> *The second rule is don't forget rule number one."*
> *—Warren Buffett*

Summary

You can't control everything. You know this. But in investing, there are some things you can control. Creating an investment plan is no different than expecting your pilot to be highly trained and your airplane to be regularly inspected: You minimize risk through careful guidelines and understanding what is in your control, while being prepared for the uncertain. Knowing what your long-term investment goals are is crucial to directing the manner in which you invest your assets.

While risk is inherent to investing, preparing for the

inevitable ups and downs of the market through strategic asset allocation can reduce your risk considerably. Lower your portfolio's volatility, and you will see more consistent gains over the long term. Minimizing risk is a strategy for long-term success, and knowing how to identify it is a powerful investing tool that is in your hands. Never forget that you have more control of your investment future outcome than you may think.

2.

Rule 2: You Can Beat the Market

*"There are two kinds of forecasters:
those who don't know, and those who don't know they don't
know."*
John Kenneth Galbraith

I grew up in Las Vegas until the age of eight, and I often spent time as a young child with my grandma, whom I called "Little Grandma" (she was little, and my other grandparents were—you guessed it—big). One day, I was at my Little Grandma's house in the kitchen helping her prepare dinner. The kitchen was small and tight, and she had one of those old electric stoves that looked like an @ symbol. When it would get hot, it would turn bright red and after being shut off the bright red would go away, but it could still be extremely hot.

One day while helping her in the kitchen, she turned on the stove. Little Grandma bent over and said to me, "Jason, make sure to never touch this stove, because even though it does not look red to you yet, that does not mean it is not hot."

Well, tell a young boy who is very curious about life not to touch something, and guess what—I did! When my grandma left the kitchen briefly to get something out of the other room, I took my hand with fingers spread apart and pressed it right down on the stove, thinking to myself, she has to be wrong. I quickly pulled it back of course, and screamed and cried for my grandma.

As soon as she walked back in the kitchen, she looked at me and said, "I told you so!" Then she put my hand under cold, running water. After getting my little hand cooled down and wrapping it in a wet cloth, she took me into her family room, sat me down, and said, "Jason, you know that your grandma loves you and wants to always protect you, right?"

"Yes, I know."

"So when I tell you not to do something, listen to me—not because I'm trying to be mean, but because I want to protect you from harm."

Why do I tell you this story? Because I can already hear what you're saying to yourself as I prepare to tell you that you cannot beat the market: "I'm the exception! I have a system, or some software, or whatever, that will enable me to outperform the market consistently, over the long term."

I'm sorry, but I'm telling you that you can't. This isn't just my opinion: History has proven this to be true. And I'm not telling you this because I'm trying to be mean, but because I, like my Little Grandma, want to protect you from financial harm. Anyone who tells you there is a strategy or financial product that is guaranteed to give you long-term above-market returns is simply misrepresenting the facts. Don't get me wrong; for most investors, professional financial services provide the oversight and smart decision-making they need to ensure the long-term profitability of their portfolios. But these strategies need to be carried out with an informed and well-established approach backed by years of data: having a strong strategic asset allocation. Again, while you can't necessarily expect to beat the market, there is significant value in portfolio management, which we are about to explore.

Active versus Passive Investing

Investment philosophy can be broken into two very broad categories: the belief that an investor, investment advisor, or fund manager can outperform the broad market as a whole by **_consistently_** picking more stock and bond winners than losers over the long term, and the belief that this cannot be done, at least not on a common or consistent enough basis to be considered a viable investment strategy. Those who adhere to the first philosophy believe in *active investing*, while those who adhere to the second philosophy believe in *passive investing*. The key is providing consistency. Again, we will be discussing the long-term data of active versus passive portfolio management as well as understanding market environments and how they play a role.

Passive investing looks to capture, not beat, the return of a particular sector of the capital markets, such as the S&P 500 or the Barclay Capital U.S. Aggregate Bond Index. This strategy is accomplished through buying and holding all of the securities that comprise the particular market, usually by purchasing index mutual funds and exchange-traded funds (ETFs). An index fund is like a basket of securities designed to represent a broad market (or a portion of the broad market). By definition, a true index fund is intended to mirror the market and thus be market capitalization weighted. An index mutual fund or ETF is assembled by purchasing the same group of securities of which the index is composed.

Indexing, therefore, refers to the strategy of matching your investments to a specific market index or benchmark. Investing in this manner provides a true opportunity for individual investors to participate, in the aggregate and at a low cost, in the performance of indices at all times.

Active investing, on the other hand, is an attempt to outperform the returns of the market through ongoing buying and selling of securities thought to be "mispriced," and/or timing security purchases and sales based on predicted market price movements.

This debate between the passive and active investing camps is long-running and often intense. Though the research and data clearly show that passive investing is the most logical philosophy for the vast majority of investors, many advocates of active investing will point to investment icon Warren Buffet as proof of their theory. These active investors and fund managers believe that their own personal skill, knowledge, and superior intellect will enable them to achieve above-market returns consistently over the long term.

Many of the greatest financial minds, writings, and theories, however, support the passive style of investing. Year after year, independent research proves that actively managed funds do not show consistency in outperforming their passively managed competition. Interestingly enough, numerous Nobel Prize winners have tried to identify the skill set needed to succeed as an active investor. Their conclusions confirm that it is nothing more than mere chance that accounts for the few who, over the short term, have managed to outperform their passive benchmarks. Not surprisingly, these same active investors could not demonstrate their "talents" with any consistency over the long term. I am not making the statement that there are no active managers out there who can beat the market. What I'm saying is that to find one to do it consistently is extremely difficult, and if you find one, it may be challenging to work with them, as they may have extremely high minimum account values.

So maybe you are asking, "What do I do then?" This does not mean that you are left alone to try to guess the best allocation. In fact, there are many talented firms that can help you create an efficient portfolio for your goals. What the research and data are saying is that trying to time the markets is not going to be a winning strategy. This approach will cause drag in your portfolio, causing you to underperform even the most basic benchmarks.

If you are not sure what investment philosophy you believe in, figure 2.1, which comes from institutional fund manager State Street Global, may be able to guide you.

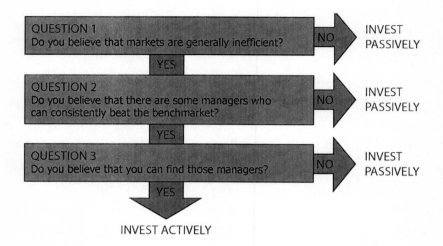

Figure 2.1   Passive versus active decision tree
Based on information provided by State Street Global Advisors

To delve deeper into the passive vs. active debate, let's go back and look at the vast amount of data that has been compiled to support the various arguments.

Mutual Funds: The Foundation of Passive Investing

We'll start by focusing on mutual fund investing and building a portfolio of mutual funds, although the arguments can be extended to portfolios of individual securities as well. Mutual funds are extremely popular because they enable individual investors to participate in ownership of hundreds of different companies without actually buying shares in all of these companies separately. As such, mutual funds can offer instant diversification, reasonable fees, and liquidity at times.

Back in 1924, the first open-end mutual fund was born: the Massachusetts Investors' Trust. It offered broad diversification of securities (at least what was considered broad at the time) that individual investors could not achieve on their own for the same cost. The fund also gave investors full liquidity in their positions. It represented an unparalleled opportunity to diversify one's portfolio at a relatively modest cost.

The investment firms that pioneered the mutual fund industry were not in the business of trying to beat the market. Rather, their mission was to focus on selecting superior securities that paid competitive dividends in order to secure profits without undue speculation, while conserving principal.

It's important to note that, at the time, there were no broad market indices like we have today, like the Standard & Poor's 500 Index or the Nasdaq Composite. There was just the Dow Jones Industrial Average, which was a price-only indicator that did not reflect the entire market of securities or the economic value, comprising thirty different large-cap stocks.[5] So the idea of trying to "beat the market" really did not exist during the early days of mutual funds.

The early mutual fund system worked well for both the financial industry and for investors for many years because it was a win-win situation. Mutual fund companies gave investors the opportunity to own shares in many different companies at a single purchase price. Think of it as buying one share of the S&P 500 Vanguard Index (VFINX) at $29.67 per share in May of 1987. Owning just this one share gives you a small piece of ownership of all 500 companies that make up that index. Investors who bought into these portfolios and the fund

5. Richard A. Ferri, *The Power of Passive Investing: More Wealth with Less Work* (Hoboken, New Jersey: Wiley), 2011.

companies that managed them did not have to worry much about losing assets when their managers failed to achieve market returns, largely because there was no one closely monitoring the fund companies the way we do today.

The issue of mutual fund performance in the early twentieth century caught the attention of Alfred Cowles III, a brilliant investing pioneer who dedicated his life to the study of economics, pushing the statistical techniques of his time. In 1932, he endowed the Cowles Foundation and dedicated it to the study of financial assets. The first recorded motto of the Cowles Commission was "Science is the Measurement."

During the mid-1920s, Cowles had subscribed to many different financial newsletters that would give investors recommendations, much like today's investment newsletters. What Cowles found to be perplexing in his research was the poor quality of the advice—and in particular, how the great bear market of 1929 to 1932 was completely missed by all the supposedly insightful investment analysis. As his curiosity took hold, Cowles began to record these recommendations from the various newsletters that were making their forecasts.

His first published report came out in 1933 in *Econometrica*, the foundation's journal, and was titled, "Can Stock Market Forecasters Forecast?" His abstract was composed of just three words: "It is doubtful."[6]

In this study, Cowles meticulously collected and analyzed different independent sources of investment advice from 1928 to 1932. The focus of the report was to determine whether these

6. Alfred Cowles, "Can Stock Market Forecasters Forecast?" *Econometrica* 1, no. 3 (1933): 309–24.

institutional investors at the time possessed the necessary skill in selecting stocks or had the ability to time the markets. His final results were nothing less than shocking: The stock-picking skills of the financial services and insurance companies were awful, and only about one-third equaled or beat the market.

Meanwhile, the performance of the newsletters, which were considered market-timers, was even worse than he suspected. Cowles discovered that investors would have been better off flipping coins than taking advice from these so-called professional investors. He found that the very best newsletter results could be obtained by random choice. But what was even more shocking was the results from the worst newsletters, which could not even be explained by chance. Put more bluntly, there was no evidence of any skill among the best newsletter writers, and the worst had, for the most, broken the laws of chance on the negative side!

Cowles followed up his initial report in 1944. The stock market crash of 1929, which was followed by the Great Depression, simply wiped out many stock investors and stock forecasting service providers by the end of the 1930s. Of the original twenty-four forecasters cited in his first report, only eleven survived. Cowles concluded that these firms failed to produce any evidence of ability to predict successfully the future course of the stock market.

In reading this piece of history you may be saying to yourself, well that was then and this is now—things are different in the twenty-first century. My response would be "Yes" and "No." Yes, the market has evolved, just as countries that were once not major global economic players are now coming onto the scene. We see this in India, China, Russia, and Portugal. Stock markets are no longer isolated to the events happening in the countries they reside in, but are becoming more sensitive to what happens to their global neighbors. Rates of correlation between previously unconnected assets are rapidly increasing, as I will discuss in Chapter 3. I have a strong feeling that the globalizing markets will continue to evolve—yes, we are in different times. The "No" is that the future is as uncertain today as it was back then. Humans will always try to find ways to build processes to help guess what markets may or may not do. So if we fast-forward another hundred years, I believe this response will still be both Yes and No. What you as an investor must do is use all of the information you can to build your portfolio. To make this clearer, let's look at the benefits of having a strong strategic passive investment methodology inside your portfolio.

The Specific Benefits of Passive Investing

Investors reap six specific benefits when adopting a passive instead of an active investing approach:

1. Lower Investing Cost
2. Superior Long-Term Performance
3. Greater Tax Efficiency
4. Broader Diversification
5. Avoidance of Portfolio Drift
6. A Framework for Emotional Self-Control

1. Lower Investing Cost
What most investors forget when it comes to the true return in

their portfolios is that *costs* are going to be paid first, and investors after that. If you are concerned about the potential return for a certain asset allocation, look first at the costs associated with the assets. Investors who invest with actively managed accounts are exposed to a number of different costs, including:

- Commissions
- Management Fees
- Bid-Ask Spreads
- Administrative Cost
- Turnover Ratio/Cost
- Market Impact
- Taxes (where applicable)

Fortunately, cost is one of the areas of investing where you as the investor have control. Specifically, you have control over whether to invest in low-cost index mutual funds and ETFs, or high-cost actively managed funds and ETFs, and whether to get investing advice from a commission-based advisor or a fee-only advisor. Very few investors truly take this into account when making portfolio decisions. Nobel Laureate William F. Sharpe drove this point home in a three-page paper he wrote in 1991: "Properly measured, the average actively managed dollar must underperform the average passively managed dollar, net of costs. Empirical analyses that appear to refute this principle are guilty of improper measurement."[7] This is not a small point. When you take into account the costs of actively managed funds, it is not mathematically possible for them to beat

7. William F. Sharpe, "The Arithmetic of Active Management," *The Financial Analysts' Journal* 47, no. 1 (1991): 7–9.

their appropriate benchmarks. Active investing costs too much to be profitable for the investor.

If your long-term goal is to have a profitable portfolio, then you must take into account the cost of active investing and discover whether that manager can get past the cost. Figure 2.2 demonstrates this point by showing two separate yield curves. Even if an actively managed fund were able to have the same distribution as its appropriate benchmark, after subtracting the stated costs, the yield curve shifts back to the actual return distribution. This leaves only a small opportunity for after-cost true value for the investor. Look at the light gray area titled "after cost." The additional cost makes it more challenging to the active managers, which brought the following observation by Sharpe: Active managers cannot mathematically beat their appropriate benchmarks.

On the other hand, by minimizing cost inside a portfolio, you place your portfolio returns closer to the market return on average, giving you a greater chance of outperforming investors who incur higher cost in their portfolios. You will spend less money, and you will make more in the long run.

When you look at the formula used to determine net return on an investment, the advantages of index fund investment are even clearer:

Net Return =
(Capital Return + Dividend/Interest Return) –
(Operating Cost + Trading Cost + Taxes)

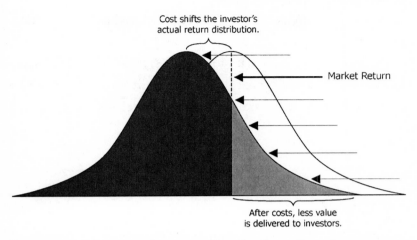

Figure 2.2 Impact of cost on distribution of market returns
Created from information compiled by The Vanguard Group

Lower costs mean a passively managed fund will outperform similar high-cost, actively managed funds.

High management fees are a major contributor to the higher cost of actively managed funds. These management fees include all the costs incurred in the internal research process—all the highly paid Ph.D.s and software engineers required to continually seek out high-yielding investment opportunities. This process generally leads to a higher turnover rate as these active managers attempt to outperform their market benchmark.

Look at figure 2.3, a breakdown of the fee differences by asset classes, to get a clearer picture of the high costs of active management. Investors in actively managed large-cap equity mutual funds in 2010, for example, were paying an average of approximately 0.89 percent (or 89 basis points) in fees annually. Investors in large-cap equity index funds were paying just 0.18 percent. And investors in an actively managed government bond fund were paying 0.54 percent. Index fund investors were paying just 0.24 percent.

Index funds operate with lower costs, regardless of the asset or sub-asset class. Because costs eat into returns, you need to evaluate them when making investment decisions.

	Actively Managed Funds (bps)	Index funds (bps)	Difference (bps)
Large-cap U.S. equity	89	18	70
Mid-cap U.S. equity	106	24	81
Small-cap U.S. equity	115	33	82
U.S. sector	105	37	68
U.S. real estate	110	26	84
International developed markets	100	31	69
International emerging markets	136	41	95
U.S. corporate bond	56	21	35
U.S. government bond	54	24	30

Note: bps = basis points

Figure 2.3   Asset-weighted expense ratios of active and index mutual funds
Research conducted by Vanguard from data provided by Morningstar, Inc. Effective date: December 31, 2010

According to a 2006 Vanguard report, a 2002 Financial Research Corporation study determined that an expense ratio was the most reliable predictor of future performance, with low-cost index funds delivering above-average performances in all of the periods examined.[8]

8. "We Believe #5," Vanguard Group, 2006, https://global.vanguard.com/ international/web/pdfs/webelieve5_042006.pdf

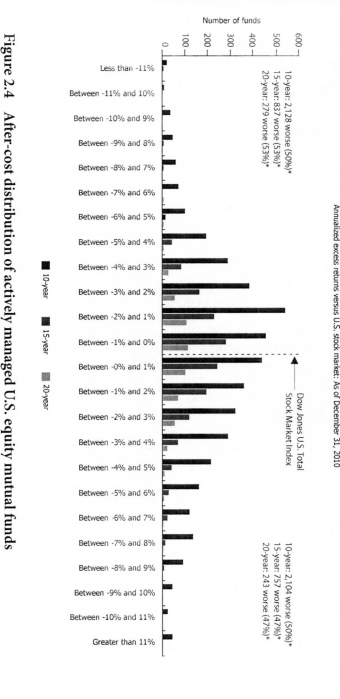

Figure 2.4   After-cost distribution of actively managed U.S. equity mutual funds

Research conducted by Vanguard from data provided by Morningstar Inc. and Dow Jones. Effective date: December 31, 2010

2. Superior Long-Term Performance

How have actively managed mutual funds performed in recent history compared to the total market index? As figure 2.4 indicates, after costs are factored in, actively managed U.S. equity mutual funds are a 50/50 shot, at best. The bars illustrate different periods of time: ten, fifteen, and twenty years.

Figure 2.5 summarizes this research. Basically, over ten-, fifteen-, and twenty-year periods, investing in actively managed U.S. equity mutual funds was the same as flipping a coin: About half over-performed and half underperformed. But when you remove the funds that were no longer in existence at the time of the study (or survivorship), the odds of over-performance shrank drastically: Between 62 percent and 72 percent of the funds underperformed.

Duration	Survivorship	Survivorship Removed
Ten Years	50%	62%
Fifteen Years	53%	67%
Twenty Years	53%	72%

Figure 2.5   Performance of actively managed U.S. equity mutual funds against market index

Created from information compiled by The Vanguard Group

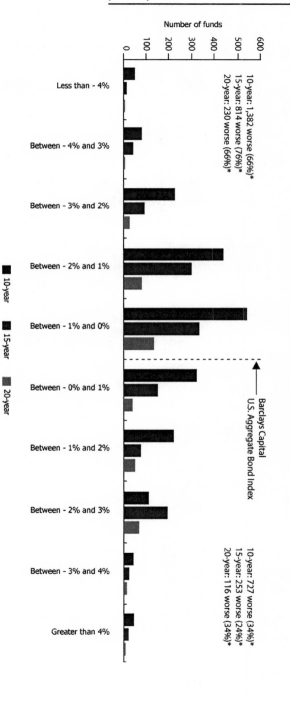

Figure 2.6 After-cost distribution of actively managed U.S. fixed income mutual funds

Created from information compiled by The Vanguard Group

The remaining mutual funds performed worse than if they had been left to complete chance. Note that these percentages do not take into account front- or back-end sales loads or taxes. If those were included in the above figures, the percentage of underperforming funds would grow even more.

The percentages get even worse when you look at actively managed fixed income mutual funds, as figure 2.6 demonstrates.

Figure 2.7 summarizes this research. Over ten-, fifteen-, and twenty-year periods, investing in actively managed U.S. fixed income mutual funds was significantly worse than flipping a coin, and worse still when you take into account the funds that were no longer in existence at the time of the study, with between 71 percent and 85 percent of the funds underperforming.

Duration	Funds still in existence at end of study	All funds included in study
Ten Years	66%	71%
Fifteen Years	76%	85%
Twenty Years	66%	81%

Figure 2.7   Percentage of actively managed U.S. fixed income mutual funds that underperformed against bond index
Created from information compiled by The Vanguard Group

Two-thirds of the surviving actively managed funds had lower returns than that of the index. Almost three-fourths of all of the funds included in the study did worse than the index. Again, these percentages do not take into account front- or back-end sales loads or taxes.

Now look at the data in annual timeframes, segmented by

asset classes. The numbers in the columns in figure 2.8 are the percentages of funds that simply underperformed their particular benchmarks in that year. Notice the dramatic percentage swings caused by the cyclical movements taking shape in the market: In 1997, 94 percent of large-value active managers underperformed their benchmarks, but in 2004 this dropped to just 29 percent. Then in 2007, the underperformance rate jumped back up to 79 percent.

Investors face considerable challenges when trying to *consistently* choose high-performing active fund managers. The only consistent thing about these data points is that active managers just cannot beat their benchmarks consistently enough to bring true value to the investor. And investors desperately seeking returns by chasing after the latest "hot" fund manager may as well be running after their own shadows. Again, I am not saying it is impossible; I am just going to echo Cowles: "It is doubtful."

To see a further illustration of average active fund managers' returns, look to figures 2.9, 2.10, and 2.11. Using the same after-cost distribution returns by actively managed funds that were noted above by asset class, the figures include the median fund excess return provided by the active fund managers. For example, as figure 2.8 indicates, 38 percent of value equity funds underperformed their benchmark (or 63 percent with survivorship removed).

The performance of active managers is drastically worse with fixed-income investments. With government bonds, for example, 94 percent of actively managed funds underperformed their benchmark (or 97 percent with survivorship removed) or value

Percentage of funds underperforming style benchmark

	1997	1998	1999	2000	2001	2002	2003	2004	2005	2006	2007	2008	2009	2010
Large value	94%	86%	94%	82%	53%	40%	39%	29%	32%	70%	79%	71%	51%	50%
Large blend	84	95	90	74	67	57	46	41	55	63	70	64	61	65
Large growth	86	99	90	62	67	55	38	50	71	63	46	57	65	76
Mid value	71	80	64	77	83	81	71	80	94	97	77	75	63	50
Mid blend	74	85	73	82	83	72	64	67	69	82	82	74	67	61
Mid growth	57	86	67	88	94	90	81	80	85	85	76	47	53	49
Small value	89	82	81	88	82	41	41	49	35	53	73	60	50	46
Small blend	46	59	69	58	54	55	50	45	60	71	81	57	63	67
Small growth	29	32	21	28	34	56	64	81	86	90	81	74	80	82

Figure 2.8 Shorter time periods and market segmentation can be highly cyclical
Created from information compiled by The Vanguard Group

provided by the average active fund manager *was actually negative: -0.77 percent.* Fund managers not only didn't add any value for the fees that were charged, but they actually subtracted value from investors!

Based on 15-years annualized returns as of 12/31/2010

	Value		Blend		Growth	
Large	38%	63%	71%	84%	64%	79%
	0.02%		-1.43%		-1.10%	
Medium	93%	96%	89%	94%	94%	97%
	-2.66%		-2.98%		-4.45%	
Small	69%	82%	89%	93%	69%	83%
	-1.18%		-3.36%		-1.38%	

■ Percentage of funds underperforming benchmark

■ Percentage underperforming, adjusted for survivorship bias

▨ Median fund excess return

Figure 2.9   Active manager returns in equity funds
Created from information compiled by The Vanguard Group

Based on 15-years annualized returns as of 12/31/2010

	Government		Corporate		GNMA		High-yield	
Short	94%	97%	96%	98%	100%	100%	87%	90%
	-0.77%		-1.49%		-0.70%		-1.10%	
Intermediate	72%	87%	85%	92%				
	-0.35%		-0.83%					

■ Percentage of funds underperforming benchmark

■ Percentage underperforming, adjusted for survivorship bias

▨ Median fund excess return

Figure 2.10   Active manager returns in fixed income funds
Created from information compiled by The Vanguard Group

Percentage of managers outperformed by benchmark and equal-weighted excess returns of active managers

International equity: 15-years annualized returns as of 12/31/2010

	Developed		Global		Emerging	
Large	30%	57%	41%	64%	65%	81%
	0.22%		-0.33%		-0.62%	

■ Percentage of funds underperforming benchmark

■ Percentage underperforming, adjusted for survivorship bias

▨ Median fund excess return

Figure 2.11   Active manager returns, by type of market
Created from information compiled by The Vanguard Group

3. Greater Tax Efficiency

Actively managed mutual fund investors can expect up to 25 percent of their annual returns to be subtracted by dividend and capital gains distributions taxes.[9] Index fund investors, however, can often avoid this sort of profit loss.

Index fund returns are less vulnerable to such taxes. Why? Because index fund managers are not constantly buying and selling securities in an attempt to beat the performance of their benchmarks. Every time a manager buys and sells securities within a fund, this may result in capital gains and dividends being distributed—and thus, capital gains taxes being assessed—to the fund shareholders, usually without them even knowing it.

According to a 2009 Vanguard report, almost half of the average actively managed fund's annual price appreciation is capital gains income.[10] While about a third of the distributions from actively managed funds are short-term capital gains and two-thirds long-term capital gains, index funds distribute only about half a percent in long-term capital gains, because index securities are sold only when the market index composition changes.

4. Broader Diversification

Passive investors enjoy broad diversification because they can cost-effectively purchase shares in a single fund that contains *all* the securities in an underlying index, such as the S&P 500.

9. Joel Dickson and John Shoven, "Taxation and Mutual Funds: An Investor Perspective," ed. James M. Poterba, *Tax Policy and the Economy, Volume 9* (Cambridge, MA: MIT Press, 1995), 151–180.
10. "The Case for Indexing," Vanguard Group, 2009, https://personal.vanguard.com/pdf/flgpi.pdf, 15.

Imagine the cost of trying to replicate the purchase of all of the companies in the S&P 500!

An index fund holds securities in the same proportion as they are held in the actual index, so when the index increases or decreases in value, the index fund's shares do as well. The only time an index fund buys or sells a stock is when the index itself changes (either in weighting or in composition). Index funds are available that track most of the benchmark markets around the world.

Consider the diversification achieved in figure 2.12, a sample portfolio of index funds. This investor has broad exposure to large- and small-cap U.S. stocks, international and emerging market stocks, bonds, and U.S. Treasury notes. While this is not a suggested portfolio, it is a brief snapshot to illustrate the broad diversification benefits that can be achieved by indexing your portfolio.

Category	Symbol	Positions Held in Fund/ETF
Large Cap	SCHX	750
Small Cap	SWSSX	960
International	SWISX	357
Emerging Markets	SFENX	359
Total Bond Market	SWLBX	838
Short Term Treasury	SCHO	39
	Total:	3,300

Figure 2.12   Sample diversified portfolio of index funds
All data was retrieved from Charles Schwab Institutional research section as of December 2011. This information can and will fluctuate.

5. Avoidance of Portfolio "Drift"

Portfolio drift occurs when an active fund manager strays away from the specific class of assets that defines the particular fund. For example, suppose you allocated 25 percent of your portfolio to a large-cap actively managed mutual fund. You are doing so with a certain risk/return expectation in mind in order to achieve your financial goals.

The fund manager, however, may have a broad mandate to purchase securities outside of this asset class in search of segments that will perform better, perhaps to purchase small- and mid-cap companies. Over time, this may cause the fund to "drift" and no longer adhere to the initial asset allocation target. Even though fund managers have well-defined mandates, they ultimate decide which securities to buy and sell in order to try to outperform their benchmark.

What you really want, however, is *consistency* in the asset style you choose to invest in—whether it is large- or small-cap stocks or anything else—to ensure the integrity of your asset allocation. Drifting inside of an active mutual fund can lead to more risk inside your portfolio. Index funds, in contrast, maintain their consistency by closely tracking the characteristics of the index to which they are pegged. Portfolio drift does not occur within index funds, because fund managers adhere to a very narrow mandate of tracking the index as closely as possible.

6. A Framework for Emotional Self-Control

This may be the most important passive investing benefit of all. Often, the biggest obstacle to our investing success is . . . ourselves.

Not surprisingly, nobody likes losing money, but everybody likes making money. Unfortunately, the emotions that are triggered when money is at stake often lead us to make very poor investment decisions. When the markets fall (and this can happen quite drastically), we tend to panic and think we should get out. When the markets rise, we worry that we're missing out on big gains, so we rush to get in.

The result? Buying high and selling low. Of course, this is the exact opposite of a winning investment strategy.

In a *Wall Street Journal* editorial on the day after the credit rating of the U.S. government was downgraded by Standard & Poor's for the first time in nearly a hundred years, Burton G. Malkiel, professor emeritus of economics at Princeton University, wrote:

> Investors who have sold out their stocks at times when there have been very large declines in the market have invariably been wrong. We have abundant evidence that the average investor tends to put money into the market at or near the top and tends to sell out during periods of extreme decline and volatility. Over long periods of time, the U.S. equity market has provided generous average annual returns. But the average investor has earned substantially less than the market return, in part from bad timing decisions.[11]

Passive investing provides a framework for self-control when it comes to making emotional investing decisions. Will the value of your portfolio go down when the benchmark that

---

11. Burton J. Malkiel, "Don't Panic about the Stock Market," *The Wall Street Journal*, August 8, 2011.

your index fund is tracking goes down? Yes, it will. But it will also go back up when that benchmark inevitably rises again. As Malkiel notes, the U.S. stock market has been a very good investment for individuals with a long-term time horizon—which is what most retirement investors should have.

Bears vs. Bulls

> *I've lost a bet. I've lost my keys. But I've never lost a decade—*
> *until now.*
> *—Sam Stovall, chief investment strategist at*
> *S&P Equity Research Services*

To look deeper into the conversation about how difficult it is to beat the markets, we must also acknowledge that all market environments are not the same. Research firms over the past several decades have identified periods of time that they call bear and bull secular market cycles. The term "secular" in the investment world means an era or an extended period of time. These are cycles that over periods of time bring either great long-term growth or periods of negative or flat growth. Most passive investment managers would argue that these cycles do not matter—just find the right allocations and hold no matter what based upon your risk profile. I believe there is great historical data that supports this approach as just mentioned in this chapter. I would also suggest that as you begin to construct your portfolio, taking into account the current environment, i.e. short-term interest rates, sovereign debt problems, demographics, or other macro issues, is being a prudent investor.

Imagine you and your portfolio are in small boat in the middle of an uncertain financial ocean that has swells of thirty-foot waves crashing into your boat, tossing you all around. This is like owning 100 percent equities in 2008 while being retired and living off the assets. The boat is the asset allocation, and the weather is the bear or bull secular market in which it is operating. Just because you like the ocean and you have great memories of sailing when it was calm, does not eliminate the fact that a storm can arise and the waves of market volatility can build up and sink your boat. Maybe you should not be in the ocean. Maybe the vessel in which you decided to cross the sea is not appropriate. As we will discover in this section, placing an understanding about potential market outcomes under the current macro environments can and will help you as an investor construct and allocate to the proper asset classes. For example: if risk seems high, you may choose to place 25 percent in the S&P 500, instead of 50 percent. You need to take the conditions into account.

A leading research firm, Crestmont, demonstrates this fluctuation over the last hundred years and states that we are currently in a bear market as of December 2011. As we have discussed, no one knows when it will end or when a long-term bull market will begin. But there is relevant macro data that should be taken into consideration as you move forward in making asset allocation decisions. The "why" behind all this is if you are reading this and retired, your time horizon for your money is much different than that of a person who is twenty-five years old and has a long time before retirement. In the next chapter, we look into this deeper when we talk about the impact of losses to someone's portfolio.

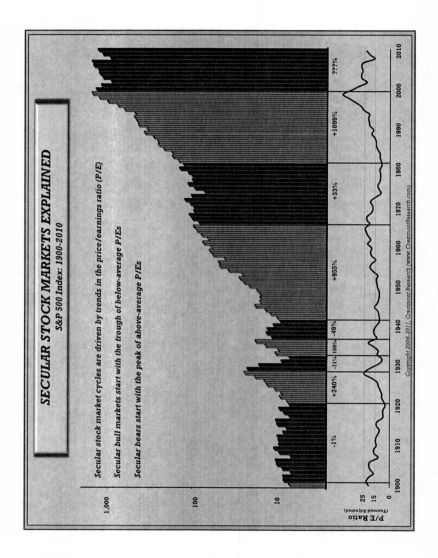

Figure 2.13   Secular stock markets explained
As presented by Crestmont Research (www.CrestmontResearch.com)

To see what markets can look like in a bear market and the kind of ride they represent, look at the chart below, which demonstrates this velocity.

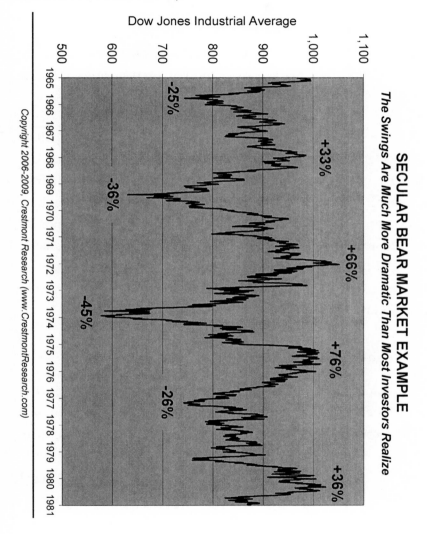

Figure 2.14   Secular bear market example
As presented by Crestmont Research (www.CrestmontResearch.com)

Look at the allocation you are seeking to deploy. How will that hold up in the different secular markets over time? Ask yourself the following questions:

- How does it affect my long-term goals?
- Can I take the market loss and stick with my allocation?
- In a bull market, does the potential upside limitation meet my goals?

Your answers to these questions will begin to give you an upside/downside range, allowing you to have a practical understanding of what that portfolio would do in the different market conditions. What I mean by an upside/downside range is simply that under extreme bull markets, how much a portfolio could make, and under extreme bear markets, how much a portfolio could lose. If you are working with an advisor, he or she should be able to tell you this information, and do not be afraid to ask, as it is extremely important.

Summary

You can't beat the market. Yes, you might find there is someone out there who has done it for a year or two. Again, anyone who tells you they are going to beat the market either has not considered the long-term performance of actively managed funds, or has insider information, making all of their decisions illegal. Like my Little Grandma told me, this may sound harsh, but I don't want you to get hurt. Don't burn your hand on the active investment stove without taking the time to do a full analysis.

Investing passively, with an understanding of the type of

environment you are operating in, will benefit the portfolio's performance. It is my opinion that a well-balanced approach that does not attempt to time the short-term market movements, but is sensitive to potential macro events, both positive and negative, will allow an investor to have a better investment experience. This statement could not be more relevant to investors who are closer to retirement, as their money turns from accumulation to distribution.

If you choose to invest under an active role, you must calculate the cost up front and weigh to see the probability of additional value brought to the portfolio. Again, we are looking to create **consistent** returns to the portfolio, and looking at all of the aspects mentioned is important if you are going down the route of having your funds actively managed.

To track the development of the passive investment model over the past couple of centuries, see the following chart. I have placed this here for those who desire to continue their research on this topic. As you will see, financial analysts and economic theorists have been advocating passive investment principles for quite some time.

Passive Investment Theories from 1863 to 2010

Date	Name	Contribution
1863	Jules Regnault	Makes the first steps toward modern stock price theory with his random walk model in *Calcul des Chances et Philosophie de la Bourse*
1900	Louis Bachelier	Publishes Ph.D. thesis, *The Theory of Speculation*, describing market prices as random and speculation as a losing battle
1934	Benjamin Graham	"[T]he investor's chief problem—and even his worst enemy—is likely to be himself." — *The Intelligent Investor*
1944	Alfred Cowles	Forecasts over the previous fifteen years "failed to disclose evidence of ability to predict successfully the future course of the stock market." — "Can Stock Market Forecasters Forecast?"
1951	John Bogle	"Time is your friend: impulse is your enemy." — *The Economic Role of the Investment Company*
1952	Harry Markowitz *1990 Nobel Prize in Economics*	In *Diversification Reduces Risk*, indicates that an optimal portfolio can be crafted for maximized returns for a given standard deviation
1958	James Tobin *1981 Nobel Prize in Economics*	In "Liquidity Preference as Behavior Toward Risk," stresses a focus on portfolio structure rather than security selection
1961	Merton Miller and Frank Modigliani *1985 and 1990 Nobel Prizes*	In "Dividend Policy, Growth, and the Valuation of Shares," declare dividend policy unreliable for selecting stocks
1965	Paul Samuelson *1970 Nobel Prize in Economics*	Declares that market prices are the best estimates of value in "Proof that Properly Anticipated Prices Fluctuate Randomly," *Industrial Management Review*

Date	Name	Contribution
1967	Michael C. Jensen	"[T]here is very little evidence that any individual fund was able to do significantly better than that which we expected from mere random chance." — "The Performance of Mutual Funds in the Period 1945-1964"
1972	Fisher Black, Myron Scholes, and Michael C. Jensen	"The Capital Asset Pricing Model: Some Empirical Tests"
1986	Gary P. Brinson, L. Randolph Hood, and Gilbert L. Beebower	In *Determinants of Portfolio Performance*, find that pension plans from 1974 to 1983 performed worse than the market index
1996	Warren Buffet	"Most investors, both institutional and individual, will find that the best way to own common stock is through an index fund that charges minimal fees. Those following this path are sure to beat the net results (after fees and expenses) delivered by the great majority of investment professionals." — annual Berkshire Hathaway report
1997	Merton Miller 1990 Nobel Prize in Economics	"There's just no sense for most [pension fund managers] to have anything but a passive investment policy." — interview with Peter Tanous, *Investment Gurus*
1998	Charles Ellis	1998 edition of *Winning the Losers Game: Timeless Strategies for Successful Strategies*
1999	John Bogle	Published book: *Common Sense on Mutual Funds: New Imperatives for the Intelligent Investor*
2000	Charles Schwab	"Most of the mutual fund investments I have are index funds, approximately 75%." — *Guide to Financial Independence*

Date	Name	Contribution
2001	William Bernstein	"The deeper one delves, the worse things look for actively managed funds." — *The Intelligent Asset Allocator*
2002	Daniel Kahneman *2002 Nobel Prize in Economics*	In response to the question "So investors shouldn't delude themselves about beating the market?" in an Associated Press interview, Kahneman replied, "They're just not going to do it. It's just not going to happen."
2002	Charles Ellis	2002 edition of book: *Winning the Losers Game: Timeless Strategies for Successful Strategies*
2008	Kenneth R. French	"Under reasonable assumptions, the typical investor would increase his average annual return by 67 basis points over the 1980 to 2006 period if he switched to a passive market portfolio." — "The Cost of Active Investing," *Journal of Finance*
2009	Niels Bekkers, Ronald Doeswijk, and Trevin Lam	"Strategic Asset Allocation: Determining the Optimal Portfolio with Ten Asset Classes," *Journal of Wealth Management*
2010	Eugene F. Fama and Kenneth R. French	"[T]he high costs of active management show up intact as lower returns to investors." — *Luck Versus Skill*
2010	John Bogle	2010 edition of *Common Sense on Mutual Funds: New Imperatives for the Intelligent Investor*
2010	Charles Ellis and Burton G. Malkiel	Publish book: *The Elements of Investing*

3.

Rule 3: High Risk Means High Return

"A prudent asset allocation that is followed by discipline will increase your chances for reaching and maintaining your financial security over your lifetime."
—Richard Ferri

One evening several years ago, my son and I went to see the San Diego Padres play. We were both excited to spend some time together and watch some good baseball. As we found our seats in the first inning, the visiting team had just made their third out.

Up come the San Diego Padres. First batter flies out. Second batter strikes out. The third batter, Adrian Gonzalez, steps up and hits a home run. The place went crazy, and my son and I were high-fiving one another.

As soon as we sat down, his first question was, "When are they going to hit another home run?"

I responded, "I'm not sure, but there is a long way to go in this game."

Well, as each inning moved on, there were no scores and no

home runs. Around the middle of the game, the other team had several base hits and doubles, ultimately winning 2-1, which is exactly how the game came to an end.

My son was truly bummed that we did not see more home runs. As a father, I felt that it was an opportunity to give a little lesson. I told my son that home runs are exciting to watch, but hitting singles and doubles are what win championships.

This lesson in baseball could not be truer when it comes to being a successful investor. Everyone likes to talk about how they bought a stock at $15 per share and now it is $45, but they will not tell you how many strikeouts it took. Swinging for the fence can sometimes involve taking on great risk inside a portfolio, which is why great risk does not always equate to great returns. Just as in baseball, there will be that occasional home run, but more often than not, it is several base hits that win the game.

Of course, investing in the stock market is a risky game. To win the game, you need to go big or go home, right? You need to take big risks, because that's the only way you'll ever make big gains, right?

Studied analysis of the stock market indicates that these assumptions can be very wrong. Big risks in your portfolio are just as likely to result in big losses as they are big gains. High risk does not always mean high return. In fact, high risk could very well mean major damage to your investments. Maybe you disagree with this idea because of risk you have taken in the past that has turned out to be very profitable for you. Great! To clarify, I am discussing market risk, not business risk. Whether high risk means high returns involves several variables. Anyone can take a risk in a stock for 12 months and sell the profits and say, "Look at me—I am smart when it comes to investing." What we are focused on in this chapter is the sustainability to produce profits. There will always be those managers or individual investors who will have their moments, but again, we are looking to establish consistency. It's simple, if you think about it. Whether markets go up or go down, these managers have no control. This is why trying to capture the market and not beat it is the only way to invest. I like to say, it is not about what you make in a period of time, but about what you keep. Many investors lose sight of this because of the emotional aspect when it comes to making money, where greed can so easily set in.

Minimizing risk simply increases your ability to avoid big swings of volatility in your portfolio, which in turn produces a more consistent return pattern. Remember what we learned about risk in the first chapter and the reason we took the time to learn how to do a diagnostic, so that you are empowered to manage risk in your portfolio.

The last decade has taught all of us many lessons when it comes to investing and the importance surrounding this topic. In this chapter, we will be discussing in more detail:

- The type of asset classes to which an investor can deploy capital
- The history of asset allocation and how it has evolved over time
- The types of strategies that are available to you when constructing the portfolio
- The importance of understanding correlations inside these asset classes

- How asset classes are changing and how they will continue to move
- Once built, how to manage the portfolio by rebalancing the importance it has to your long-term performance

Remember this: *How you allocate your assets is the single most important factor in your portfolio's long-term profitability.* By including a variety of asset classes and continually reevaluating them to ensure your overall portfolio is balanced, you will find there are some things you can be sure of when you are investing in most market environments.

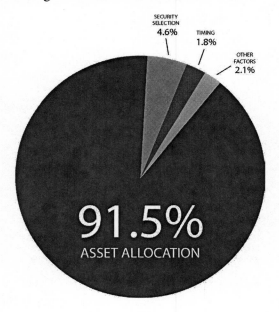

Figure 3.1 Allocating portfolio assets for long-term profitability
Created from information presented by Genworth Financial Wealth Management, Inc., from data compiled by Brinson, Hood, and Beebower, Financial Analysts Journal, 1988 and Brinson, Singer, and Beebower, Financial Analysts Journal, 1991.

The importance of asset allocation to investors' returns has been well researched and documented. One of the landmark studies conducted by some of the world's most revered investment experts studied the returns of ninety-one large pension funds from 1974 through 1983. The focus of the research was to measure scientifically which factors were most important in determining investment performance. The results of their research fundamentally reshaped how investors manage money. They found, on average, that more than 91 percent of a portfolio's variance comes from asset allocation. The traditional areas where investors focus their time and attention, selecting individual securities, explained surprisingly little of the return variations. This can be seen in figure 3.1. This is a huge chunk of the pie that cannot be ignored. How you allocate your assets is by far the most important determinant of how profitable your portfolio will be.

History of Asset Allocation

While most people would agree that you shouldn't put all of your eggs in one basket, no one had provided a consistent method of investing according to this old saying when Harry Markowitz sat down to write his dissertation. Markowitz, a student at the University of Chicago in the early 1950s, set out to devise a mathematical calculation that took into account probable risk in relation to an optimized investment portfolio.

At the time, investment philosophies focused on establishing the risk of individual securities and crafting a portfolio based on those deemed to provide the best return. Such a philosophy, however, did not prevent an investor from, say, deciding that because automobiles were a relatively low risk, he would invest in a slew of car companies and consider his portfolio poised to profit greatly. Markowitz knew that there had to be a way to quantify this insight into an equation that would represent relative risk across asset classes. The result was modern portfolio theory. Markowitz, who won the Nobel Prize in Economics in 1990, described the development of modern portfolio theory in the following manner:

> The basic concepts of portfolio theory came to me one afternoon in the library while reading John Burr Williams's *Theory of Investment Value.* Williams proposed that the value of a stock should equal the present value of its future dividends. Since future dividends are uncertain, I interpreted Williams's proposal to be to value a stock by its expected future dividends. But if the investor were only interested in expected values of securities, he or she would only be interested in the expected value of the portfolio; and to maximize the expected value of a portfolio one need invest only in a single security. This, I knew, was not the way investors did or should act. Investors diversify because they are concerned with risk as well as return. Variance came to mind as a measure of risk. The fact that portfolio variance depended on security covariances added to the plausibility of the approach. Since there were two criteria, risk and return, it was natural to assume that investors selected from the set of Pareto optimal risk-return combinations.[12]

---

12. Harry Markowitz, "Harry M. Markowitz – Autobiography," Nobelprize.org, accessed October 25, 2011, http://www.nobelprize.org/nobel_prizes/economics/laureates/1990/markowitz-autobio.html

Most investors understand that a portfolio filled with large-cap stocks that individually are considered low risk can actually, on the whole, be a risky holding. A small drop in this asset class could wreak havoc on such a blend of investments. What is more, that drop in large-cap stocks might be strongly correlated with the rise in another asset class. Perhaps fixed income rises when large-cap stocks fall. Markowitz's portfolio theory accounts for this. A diversified portfolio that includes both large-cap stocks and fixed income is much stronger in the long run than a collection of stocks that rise and fall together.

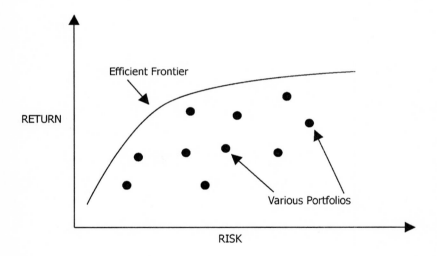

Figure 3.2 The Efficient Frontier

Part of Markowitz's work was the development of the efficient frontier. The efficient frontier is a graphed line that indicates the set of optimal portfolios for a given return. This line can be seen in figure 3.2 that starts in the lower quadrant and arcs to the upper right. The other dots labeled "various portfolios" are made of up different asset class that, when calculated, are not optimized. Simply stated, these portfolios are taking more risk with less possible return. Anyone would say that is not a good deal, and a change to the portfolio needs to take place. This is best illustrated in figure 3.3.

An efficient frontier graph illustrates the point at which the maximal profitability can be reached with the most minimal risk possible for that level of expected return.

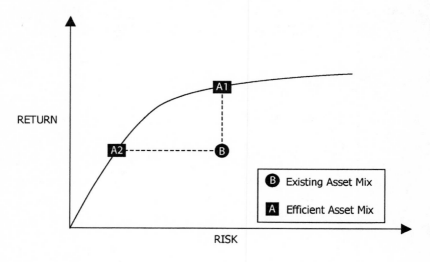

Figure 3.3   Example portfolio on the Efficient Frontier

To better understand the importance of why an investor would want a portfolio to be sitting on the efficient frontier, look at figure 3.3. There are three portfolios: A_1, A_2, and B. Let's assume they are composed of multiple asset classes. Using Markowitz calculations, we come to find portfolios A_1 and A_2 are truly optimized for the risk/return ratio, and this is why you find them plotted on top of the frontier. Portfolio B, using the same Markowitz calculation process, is telling us a different story. This portfolio is actually taking the same amount of risk as portfolio A_1 (again measured by its standard deviation) with a much lower expected rate of return. This diagnostic gives the investor excellent information and two fundamental options to improve the risk/return ratio. Option one, A_1 on the graph, is to take the same risk as the portfolio is currently structured to absorb but make changes to the allocation. Option two, A_2 on the graph, would be to reduce the risk in the portfolio by sliding it to the left and making the allocation sit on the curve.

There are many software programs in the marketplace using this principle to help you map a myriad of combinations of portfolio possibilities and pinpoint the line along which the most efficient portfolios can be found. There is caution that I must state here when looking at applying software on your own or even with an advisor. There are many variables that go into it, enough that entire books have been written about it. Without getting into it deeply here, I can tell you that this is an area in which I would look to a firm that has institutional experience in using the technology tools available.

"Markowitz came along, and there was light," said William F. Sharpe, the creator of the Capital Asset Pricing Model, in a 1998 interview. "Markowitz said a portfolio has expected return and risk. Expected return is related to the expected return of the securities, but risk is more complicated. Risk is related to the risks of the individual components as well as the correlations.

"That makes risk a complicated feature, and one that human

beings have trouble processing. You can put estimates of risk/ return correlation into a computer and find efficient portfolios. In this way, you can get more return for a given risk and less risk for a given return, and that's efficiency a la Markowitz."[13]

Markowitz's basic efficient frontier has been expanded and improved upon by many theorists since the 1950s. Sharpe himself was one of these theorists. As a doctoral student in the early 1960s, Sharpe approached Markowitz for assistance in crafting his dissertation topic. Markowitz encouraged him to explore portfolio theory on his own terms, and soon Sharpe was pursuing what would become the Capital Asset Pricing Model (CAPM). Sharpe described the sources of the model in the following manner:

> The CAPM comes out of two things: Markowitz, who showed how to create an efficient frontier, and James Tobin, who in a 1958 paper said if you hold risky securities and are able to borrow—buying stocks on margin—or lend—buying risk-free assets—and you do so at the same rate, then the efficient frontier is a single portfolio of risky securities plus borrowing and lending, and that dominates any other combination.[14]

The CAPM, in part, boils portfolio theory down to a concept termed "beta." If you remember, we talked about beta and its role inside your portfolio in Chapter 1. Beta is essentially the relationship of a given security to the movement of the overall

---

13. Qtd. in Jonathan Burton, "Revisiting the Capital Asset Pricing Model," *Dow Jones Asset Manager* (May/June 1998), 20–28.
14. Ibid.

market. It describes the extent to which a security correlates to the market as a whole, providing a description of risk. Sharpe's work went against the grain of the prevailing investment notions of the 1960s, but the CAPM remains a widely used approach to this day. Further, Sharpe is an avowed proponent of passive investing: "You can't beat the average; net of costs, the returns for the average active manager are going to be worse."[15]

More recently, other investment minds have been working on ways to improve the practical limitations of Markowitz's theoretical efficient frontier. Richard and Robert Michaud, in the late 1990s and early 2000s, developed what they termed and patented Resampled Efficiency.™ Resampled Efficiency builds upon the work of Markowitz and other theorists by adding newer technology and the insights of the last fifty years of stock market shifts to provide more accurate and ultimately more profitable portfolios. Briefly, Resampled Efficiency adds the element of the future markets' uncertainty into the equation, providing multiple alternative portfolio scenarios that can be mapped along a resampled efficiency frontier. It takes these uncertain scenarios and runs multiple outcomes to come up with an average to create a new efficient frontier. The effects of this aggregated portfolio mapping are more optimized results, better shaped to reflect how the market actually functions.

Resampled Efficiency takes uncertainty into account by calculating scores of possible outcomes for given portfolios. For example, imagine you are at a football game. At the beginning of play, instead of flipping the coin once, the referee decides to flip the coin a hundred times. If you flip a fair coin once, the

---

15. Ibid.

chances of it landing on heads or tails will always be 50/50. But if you flip a coin a hundred times to determine a winner, you might get seventy heads and thirty tails, or forty-three heads and fifty-seven tails, or fifty-two heads and forty-eight tails. The actual outcome of such a sample size of coin tosses is rarely going to be exactly fifty and fifty.

Michaud and Michaud's work acknowledges that we cannot know the exact outcome of the future, even if we have a given probability. Because we cannot know the exact scenario of how stocks are going to perform, we want to bring in a variety of types of markets and average out the possibilities that these markets represent. The challenge with Markowitz's theory is it takes into account only the initial probability. At the football game, imagine someone saying the outcome of a hundred coin tosses is guaranteed to be fifty heads and fifty tails, every time. In theory, this would be the outcome. But in practice, this just doesn't happen. Investments work in much the same way, as I am sure many would attest to. Resampled Efficiency, by taking into account the inherent instability of markets, gives you a higher probability of achieving your targeted returns with less risk, or less standard deviation. The importance is obvious— if you are creating your financial goals around your portfolio, you want to give yourself the best chance for success, and that is how a resampled efficient frontier can add value.

Harry Markowitz broke the theoretical ground on which today's practical investing approaches now rest. Investment minds since then have built models and strategies that allow investors to allocate their assets in more and more effective ways. The focus on finding optimal asset allocation will always be a work in progress, but the strides to help investors in the last several decades can be a tremendous help to you, if applied properly.

Asset Allocation Defined

With so much talk about asset allocation up to this point in the book, it would make sense to lay it out for you to understand. For some this may be review, and for others it will be brand new. Whatever camp you are in, I encourage you to read through this.

Asset allocation is, in its most basic sense, where you put your money. To use a metaphor, it is the ingredients of the cake you decided to bake. Where you invest, and the extent to which you invest in diverse asset classes, determines the bulk of your potential profitability. To avoid exposing your portfolio to serious vulnerability, you must allocate your assets in classes diverse enough that major fluctuations in a single sector will not overturn your portfolio completely. But to do this, you have to understand what makes a portfolio diverse. What makes this difficult is that what used to be a diverse portfolio, in previous markets, is not nearly as diverse today.

Asset classes can be divided into three major categories: equities, fixed-income, and cash equivalents. Equities include all forms of stocks. Fixed-income assets are typically bonds. Cash equivalents include money market instruments and Treasury bills as well as cash itself. These three categories in turn can be broken down further into subcategories. Figure 3.4 shows a detailed risk/return pyramid and where these assets have historically been placed. As a disclosure: Asset classes can and do move, so what is in one category does not guarantee any results of a future performance risk situation.

- Equities denote partial ownership in a company and represent shareholders' profits. Equities are by far the riskiest asset class, especially in the short term. The fluctuation of the stock market means major gains and major losses can occur in very small timeframes. Subcategories of equities include small cap and large cap stocks, international stocks, mutual funds, variable annuities, options, and futures.

- The category of fixed-income assets encompasses varying types of bonds, which are securities with set repayment schedules. Fixed-income assets do not carry risk to the same extent that equities do, so the potential gains from these assets are smaller, but the potential losses are as well. Subcategories of fixed-income assets include government-issued securities, corporate-issued securities, inflation-protected securities, mortgage-backed securities, and asset-backed securities.

- Cash equivalent assets carry the least risk of fluctuation, but gains in this class are typically so small that little profit can be realized from them. Inflation often takes care of any potential gains. Subcategories of cash equivalents include cash deposits, money market funds, fixed annuities, and Treasury bills.

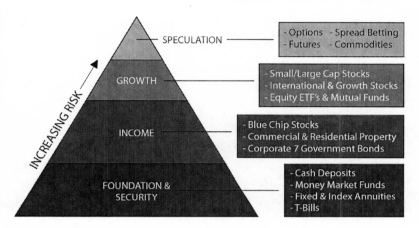

Figure 3.4   The investment pyramid

Another way of understanding asset classes is by visualizing them stacked in an investment pyramid as seen in figure 3.4. At the bottom of the pyramid, the foundation, are the most unchanging asset categories: cash deposits, money market funds, fixed annuities, and Treasury bills. These are the secure base on which a portfolio is built. Just above the foundation is the middle of the pyramid, income. Here can be found blue chip stocks, commercial and residential property, and corporate and government bonds. Slightly more risky than the foundation, the income categories form the relatively stable center of the pyramid. Above these is the growth section, in which small cap and large cap stocks, as well as equity mutual funds and variable annuities are placed. These investment options carry more risk, and so they rest upon the more solid categories below them. The tiny top of the pyramid is made of speculation assets: options, futures, spread betting, commodities, and currencies. As speculation is the riskiest section, it forms the smallest part of a strongly grounded pyramid. The key takeaway here is to visualize the general attributes of these asset classes and the potential risk/return they might bring.

Building a Portfolio

So how do you create a balanced portfolio to meet your goals? To keep this simple and straightforward, one of the first steps that an investor should take is to determine the degree of risk inside the portfolio. This can be done in several different ways, and there are many different resources available to you. This is an area where a skilled and qualified advisor can bring tremendous value to you. For illustrative purposes, I have included a great resource from State Street Global, which created the different groups that are shown in figure 3.5. These are labeled 1-7. As you read across and down, your goal is to find the statement that you best identify with. The chart provides a recommended target asset allocation for each group. For example, a Group 3 investor would have 75 percent fixed income and 25 percent equity-type assets.

Once an investor has established his or her long-term target allocation, then making the decision on how to implement and manage it moving forward will be the next important step.

Asset Allocation Approaches

There are two main approaches you can take to create a balanced portfolio successfully. There is one strategy that I believe is more efficient, but I want to educate you on both so you clearly understand the difference. The first, strategic asset allocation, involves periodic rebalancing with a long-term aim.

ATTRIBUTES	GROUP 1	GROUP 2	GROUP 3	GROUP 4	GROUP 5	GROUP 6	GROUP 7
	RISK AVERSE						
ATTITUDE TOWARDS RISK	Risk equals danger to these investors, who have little confidence in their ability to make good financial decisions.	Risk equals danger or uncertainty; investors in this group adapt to poor decisions uneasly	Risk relates to uncertainty, yet they are prepared to take a small to medium degree of risk in their investments. They are usually confident in their decisions.	Risk represents uncertainty to these investors. They have a reasonable amount of confidence in their ability to make good financial decisions.	Risk equals opportunity and a degree of risk is acceptable. They have a reasonable amount of confidence in their ability to make good financial decisions.	Risk equates to opportunity, a large degree of risk is an opportunity or thrill, and they have complete confidence in their ability to make good financial decisions.	These investors think of risk as an opportunity or thrill, and they have a great deal of confidence in their ability to make good financial decisions.
FINANCIAL PROFILE	Always more concerned with possible losses than possible gains.	More concerned with possible losses than possible gains.		Still usually more concerned with possible losses than possible gains.	More concerned with possible gains than possible losses.		Always more concerned with possible gains than possible losses.
	Capital Preservation	Moderate Conservative	Moderate	Moderate Growth	Growth		Maximum Growth
	100%	90% / 10%	75% / 25%	50% / 50%	75% / 25%		100%

■ INCOME   ■ GROWTH

Figure 3.5 Finametrica Scale of Investor Risk Profiles

Created from information provided by State Street Global. The portfolios that are associated with the different groups are not from State Street Global, but from the author as an example. These are not recommended portfolios.

The second, tactical asset allocation, involves rebalancing to take advantage of short-term gains to seek underpriced securities. This approach is more often found in an active investor. I want to speak to both methodologies to further educate you so that you can recognize it better when working with your advisors and determine which you believe is best for your future.

Strategic Asset Allocation

Strategic asset allocation simply takes a long-term perspective to the marketplace and does not adjust the asset range that often. Investors under this strategy would do their homework on the front side to identify the right mix of stock, bonds, and other asset classes. Rebalancing is key to strategic asset allocation, and this rebalancing occurs in an effort to maintain the original asset class allocations in a portfolio. A strategically balanced portfolio is managed through periodic evaluations of respective asset classes' profitability. If one asset class is gaining disproportionately in relation to the other asset classes in a portfolio, assets are redistributed to regain the original proportions. Say, for instance, you begin with 10 percent of your portfolio in the speculation segment of the investment pyramid, 30 percent in the growth segment, 50 percent in the income segment, and 10 percent in the foundation segment. Imagine your speculation investments begin to earn significant profits, doubling their share in your allocation to 20 percent. When it comes time to rebalance your portfolio, you would redistribute your assets to recover the percentages of your original division, moving enough of your assets out of the speculation segment to restore the balance.

These distribution rates do not necessarily remain constant, however. A significant part of a strategic asset allocation approach is analyzing and identifying the proper allocation among asset classes, and this may change over time. "To form a long-term portfolio, investors must first think systematically about their preferences and about the constraints they face," said Harvard economics professor John Y. Campbell, in a 2002 address. "[I]nvestors must form beliefs about the future—not just about average asset returns and risks, but about the dynamic processes that determine interest rates and risk premia. These beliefs must be consistent with some reasonable view about the equilibrium of the economy."[16] How you understand markets to function, and how markets actually do function, can and probably will shift during the life of your portfolio. For this reason, a strategic approach must remain firm but flexible. This statement by professor Campbell speaks to what was discussed earlier about markets that move in bear and bull secular markets. I believe he is not suggesting becoming an active investor, but rather an intelligent one by making sure that your beliefs and emotions are in check with the reality surrounding your investments. This is done by taking into consideration the fact that the asset allocation strategies used in 1990 may not produce the same results in 2012.

Tactical Asset Allocation

A tactical asset allocation approach to investment operates under a much different methodology. A TAA strategy is in

---

16. John Y. Campbell, "Strategic Asset Allocation: Portfolio Choice for Long-Term Investors" (Invited address to the American Economic Association and American Finance Association, Atlanta, Georgia, January 4, 2002).

constant search to find asset classes that are deemed to be underpriced so that the investor can buy low and sell when the perceived profits have reached a peak in a certain period of time. Tactical allocation strives to maximize profitability through careful periodic redistribution of asset classes. Within certain set parameters, a portfolio's mix of assets is allowed to fluctuate to take advantage of market price shifts. There are many different tactical methodologies in the marketplace today, all of which are driven off of two main inputs. The managers are fundamental managers or technical managers or, in some cases, a combination. A manager who uses a fundamental approach looks at the underline of a company or sector. How are their profits, future product launch, management, and other structural fundamentals? For example, is the Apple iPad going to beat out the competition?

Managers using a technical approach are not interested in any of that and look rather at data to see if a market is going to break out to the upside or downside. They are not interested in what management is doing, but rather in what charts are looking like on a computer screen. They are taking historical charts and comparing them to current ones to help decide when to move in and out of positions.

When those gains have been attempted, however, the portfolio is returned to its target allocation proportions. If, for instance, stocks were thought likely to perform well in the near future, a tactical asset allocator would move assets into stocks temporarily, until the target result was obtained. At that point, the portfolio would be returned to its original distribution. This movement of assets based on key market shifts has the

potential to provide greater gains than a strategic asset allocation approach, but it also carries more risks.

It is not easy to predict the perfect allocation mix. A 2010 report by the Vanguard Group concluded that while, if done well,
tactical asset allocation can be profitable, the approach is not
often carried out profitably: "Our results show that while some
TAA strategies have added value, on average, TAA strategies
have not consistently produced excess returns. . . . [S]uccess-
ful TAA requires rigorous methodology."[17] To come out ahead
with a tactical asset allocation approach, your assets have to
shift at key moments, and the shifts your assets make may not
always capture your targeted short-term gains. You see this
type of portfolio execution at the institutional level where they
have the qualification and resources to support it.

Hybrid Asset Allocation

We all know what a hybrid is, taking a piece of two separate
things or ideas to create one new thing. In this case, com-
bining strategic and tactical asset allocation means you will
apply a low-cost ETF passive model, wrapped with a quantitative process to identify mispriced assets. The thought of
a tactical manager is that all markets exhibit some level of
inefficiencies over time, which means asset classes become
mispriced, creating investable opportunities. Strategies that
are executed like this can bring the value of being nimble in
uncertain market environments embraced by political unrest,
like we saw in 2011.

What you will find in the investment industry is that there

17. Kimberly A. Stockton and Anatoly Shtekhman, "A Primer on Tactical
Asset Allocation Strategy Evaluation," Vanguard Research, July 2010.

○

are different methodologies out there, but at the end of the day they will fall into three different camps:

1. 100 percent Strategic Allocation
2. 100 percent Tactical Allocation
3. Hybrid Strategic Allocations

Take the time to find out from your advisor or money manager which of these three categories they would fall into.

Correlation between Asset Classes

Through a careful blend of asset classes, you can craft a portfolio that provides gains over time, without undue risk to your investment capital. But key to creating this blend is understanding what makes a diverse portfolio in today's markets. Recent market analysis indicates certain equities and other asset classes have become more dependent upon one another. This information goes against what most planners have been using for decades when they build portfolios for their clients. What this means is that when these equities fall, other asset classes fall as well. This is known as correlation. When asset classes become correlated, their profitability becomes intertwined, and a portfolio that contains them can quickly become exposed to significant risk. The recent correlation trend among certain asset classes necessitates a more careful approach to asset allocation and portfolio rebalancing.

Genworth Financial Wealth Management compiled a recent report that charted the correlation trend among certain asset classes. This report indicated that in a relatively short period of time, from the early 1990s to the early 2000s, many

1990 - 1999

	US LC	US SC	Int'l Dev.	Int'l EM	REITs	Fixed Inc.	Cash
US LC	1						
US SC	0.78	1					
Int'l Dev.	0.54	0.44	1				
Int'l EM	0.57	0.60	0.53	1			
REITs	0.45	0.63	0.25	0.33	1		
Fixed Inc.	0.41	0.18	0.19	0.00	0.27	1	
Cash	0.00	-0.08	-0.14	-0.12	-0.10	-0.14	1

2000 - June 2010

	US LC	US SC	Int'l Dev.	Int'l EM	REITs	Fixed Inc.	Cash
US LC	1						
US SC	0.81	1					
Int'l Dev.	0.87	0.79	1				
Int'l EM	0.79	0.76	0.88	1			
REITs	0.61	0.67	0.60	0.52	1		
Fixed Inc.	-0.04	-0.05	0.06	0.02	0.13	1	
Cash	-0.04	-0.06	-0.06	-0.10	-0.01	0.06	1

US LC - US Large Cap, represented by S&P 500; US SC - US Small Cap, represented by Russell 2000
Int'l Dev - International Developed, represented by MSCI EAFE; Int'l EM - International Emerging, represented by MSCI Emerging Markets
REIT's - REIT's, represented by FTSE Nareit Equities; Fixed Inc - US Fixed Income, represented by Barclays Capital US Aggregate
Cash - Cash, represented by Citigroup 3 month T-Bill

Source: Zephyr Style Advisor

Figure 3.6   Ten-year correlations of asset classes
Created from information presented by Genworth Financial Wealth Management, Inc., from data compiled by Zephyr Style Advisor

equities that had been independent from one another had begun to move closer and closer together. Between U.S. and international large cap stocks, for instance, the correlation rate almost doubled: "[W]hile in the 1990s these two asset classes only moved in the same direction a little more than half of the time, during the most recent decade they moved in the same direction nearly nine times out of 10."[18] Such increased correlation turns balanced portfolios into investment nightmares if one is not aware of this information. If these equities perform poorly at the same time, nine times out of ten, a portfolio that contains them will be receiving a major pummeling nine times out of ten.

This chart from Genworth Financial Wealth Management clearly illustrates the shift in correlation rates provides more detail for this trend. If we look at the international developing (Int'l Dev.) in figure 3.6, markets jumped from a 0.54 and 0.44 correlation with U.S. large-cap and small cap stocks, respectively, to a stunning 0.87 and 0.79, respectively. This near doubling occurred within the span of a couple of decades. These trends don't end here, either. Correlations from just 10 years ago are moving closer and closer. This means that the assumptions you made in 2000 could very well be becoming riskier. You might think you are safe, but it's quite possible you're not as safe as you were in 2000. If there is no wide separation in the correlation between asset classes in a portfolio, then that portfolio has drifted dangerously out of balance.

There are many reasons for such increased rates of correlation.

---

18. Genworth Financial Wealth Management, Inc., "Diversifying Portfolios for Early 21st Century Markets," Pleasant Hill, CA, 2010.

For international and domestic stocks, Genworth cites global-ization: "One reason for larger positive correlations among stocks may be the fact that equity markets have become highly interdependent as company operations have become increas-ingly global."[19] It is clear that as markets shift, investment strat-egies have to shift, too. The basic principle of asset allocation remains the same. But the manner in which assets are allo-cated, or the weighting in each asset class, has to be flexible. A good example: As I am writing this book, the 10-year trea-sury is around 2 percent. Historically speaking, this cannot go much lower, so taking that into account when looking at fixed income, i.e. bonds and the duration associated to them, would be important. I do not believe flexibility equals active manage-ment. I believe flexibility equals intelligent investing.

Because correlation is unpredictable as the future of the stock market, it can wreak havoc with a portfolio. In an anal-ysis of correlation between a variety of asset classes and the S&P 500 over the course of thirty-five years, William J. Coaker maintains that the severity of asset correlation is underesti-mated by most investors. Coaker presents some of his find-ings, such as the increased correlation throughout the 1990s between both international markets and emerging markets in relation to the S&P 500, and concludes that correlation cannot be extrapolated from previous performances: "Market periods and relationships appear unique, not an average of the past."[20] New trends can arise seemingly out of nowhere, and investors

---

19. Ibid.
20. William J. Coaker, Jr., "The Volatility of Correlation: Important Impli-cations for the Asset Allocation Decision," *Journal of Financial Planning* 19, no. 2 (February 2006): 58–69.

sometimes have to reevaluate their approaches to accommo-
date these macro changes.

A major component of this reevaluation is focusing on
implementing strategies that are nimble to markets, rather
than a historically static strategy for asset allocation. Indeed,
the historical movement of markets can offer little in the way
of instruction for future investments: "The correlation among
asset classes appears to be inherently unstable. Unstable relationships complicate the asset allocation decision. The conventional practice of using historical correlations relies on relationships in the past being the same in the future, which is not
correct."[21] Analysis of the last decades of market information
indicates asset correlation cannot be predicted, and nor will
they ever be predicted. Historical data from past market performance are useful in planning future investments, but only
to the extent that they reveal the constantly changing nature of
assets and their correlation to one another. The key takeaway
from this is for you to know and understand that when building your portfolio, the overall correlation inside the combination of all of the asset classes that we see today will most likely
change over time. This is why having a routine check-up on
your portfolio to identify if you need to change the weightings
in your asset classes is important.

Rebalancing Should Be a Priority

Building an efficient portfolio, as you have come to learn, has
a lot of moving pieces. Once done, you might say, "Glad that is
over" so that you can move on. This is wrong, because once you

_____

21. Ibid.

invest your portfolio, the asset classes grow and shrink based upon the market. If you are using a strategic allocation strategy, then rebalancing is a major priority for you. If you are deploying a tactical allocation strategy, the rebalancing is not as critical because the managers are trying to seek returns wherever the markets are driving.

You simply cannot expect your portfolio to stay static, because markets do not stay static. Having a rebalancing strategy follows the principle of buying low and selling high by trimming a portfolio's exposure to assets that have performed well and reinvesting the proceeds in assets that have been performing more weakly. If executed properly, it can help reduce portfolio risk and enhance returns over time.

So why do many investors not apply this principle to their portfolio? One main reason is because the process is emotionally counterintuitive. Having a disciplined rebalancing strategy can help you control your emotions while potentially enhancing your risk/return ratio in the portfolio. There are many different beliefs about when is the most optimal time to rebalance. Some money managers will suggest a target range trigger. Consider the following example to see this in action. Assume you have a $1,000,000 portfolio to invest and you want a long-term target asset mix of 50 percent stocks and 50 percent bonds. So you would have $500,000 in stocks and $500,000 in bonds. If over the next year your stock investments gain 20 percent and your bonds were flat, your stock portfolio would increase to $600,000 and your bonds to $400,000. To regain your desired 50/50 mix, you would need to sell those profits and buy back into the bonds at a lower price. The focus here is to determine what will be the trigger for you or your advisor to sell and bring the portfolio back to the target 50/50 allocation. This is something that you or your advisor needs to spell out in the beginning of the investment relationship. The other strategy that is used is simply time, which is usually associated to a monthly, quarterly, or annual basis.

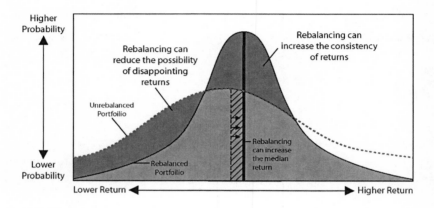

Figure 3.7   The potential advantages of rebalancing
Created from information presented by AllianceBernstein Investment Research and Management

Where is the value in rebalancing? Figure 3.7 shows that rebalancing changes the shape of portfolio risk. As the superimposed bell curves in this chart indicate, a well-balanced portfolio provides significantly increased stability and potential value. By reducing the probability of widely variant returns (lowering the outer shoulders of the bell curve), rebalancing a portfolio increases the chances that investment returns will be realized. By minimizing risk, a rebalanced portfolio shifts the probable median return toward higher levels. A lower probability of extreme highs and lows in a portfolio creates a more stable and sure investment strategy. A higher median means a greater chance of profitability.

It may seem reasonable to simply invest your money and leave the rest up to the winds of the financial markets. When asset classes perform well or decrease in their value, they shift the distribution inside your portfolio. Failing to rebalance can take you off course as you begin to experience more risk than originally desired. On the other hand, when you have a disciplined approach to rebalancing your portfolio, you can enhance your long-term returns and ultimately help provide a smoother ride along the way.

Summary

Hitting home runs in the financial world is fun, just like it was fun for my son to see Adrian Gonzalez hit one out of the park at the baseball game. What is not fun is watching all the strike-outs and pop flies that do not produce results. Do not get distracted by the big win, but build a portfolio that is going to give you consistent returns. I hope you are starting to see a pattern emerging for you in your investment life.

So what is the most important decision an investor makes? I hope by now you can answer this question quickly: asset allocation. Again, how you allocate your assets is the single most important factor in your portfolio's long-term profitability. Do not get pulled in with trying to hit financial home runs in order to achieve your financial goals. Be the investor who gets really good at hitting singles and doubles, and over time watch your money grow for you and your future. As discussed in this chapter and the previous one, there is a lot that goes into making that happen, from building the portfolio, to managing the portfolio and monitoring the correlations of the assets that you place inside your portfolio. Now that you are equipped with this information, you are already in a position to increase your wealth.

4.

Rule 4: Control Your Emotions

---

*"The investor's chief problem—and even his worst enemy—is
likely to be himself."*
Benjamin Graham

Maybe this comes across as a surprise, but I love the
store Bed Bath and Beyond. I know that I am most
likely not their target demographic, but they have
the coolest stuff. There is one right by my house. One day after stopping by the bank, I decided to go in for a quick walk
around the store. As I was walking through the kitchen section,
I came across the blenders, and right in front of me was the
blender of all blenders. The Ninja!

This blender can do it all. I had seen the infomercials, and
I was thinking to myself how I would be able to do so much at
home if I had this blender. I could make great smoothies, cre-
ative sauces for chicken . . . I needed this blender. What made it
even better was that it was on sale for 20 percent off! How could
I pass it up, right? So, thinking how the blender was going to
change my life, I decided to buy it. I took it home and showed

my wife, and she knew that give it a couple weeks, and it would find a place deep in our cabinet, maybe never to see the light of day again. Well, that first night I was whipping up all sorts of things. It was a great blender. It still is a great blender. As I tell this story, I have used that blender twice.

I know I'm not the only one who has ever made an emotional decision when buying a product. We are emotional creatures. All too often, emotions in the market are what cause great loss and anxiety to an investor.

What makes financial markets move is you. Yes, you and millions of other emotionally driven investors buying and selling to try to find profits. This is why I am sure you've heard this before: "Just control your emotions." Markets go up, and markets go down, but as long as you keep a clear head, you'll be fine. Or so a certain mindset seems to say.

But new findings in psychology and science have shot that mindset to pieces. When markets fluctuate, humans have unavoidable physiological responses. This field of study is called behavioral finance, which applies the study of psychology to the investment process. Behavioral finance seeks to explain the role of emotions in investors' actions. It is an extremely useful and respected method to help determine where investors go wrong with their investment decisions. Two early pioneers in the field, Princeton University's Daniel Kahneman and George Mason University's Vernon Smith, received the 2002 Nobel Prize in Economics for their behavioral finance research. They found that the circuitry in our brains is "wired" in ways that cause us to make costly investment mistakes.[22] The bottom line is that it is normal for us to get emotional, second-guess our allocation, and ultimately make inappropriate changes to our portfolios that affect the overall returns.

We panic, we anchor, we herd, we overreact, and we make poor investment decisions. As you weigh the evidence in this chapter, I believe you will quickly come to see, as I have, that we simply cannot control our emotions. What we can do, however, is mitigate their influence **<u>by managing them</u>**. To invest successfully, we cannot expect to gain control over our emotional responses—biology is just too a great a force to go up against. But by knowing ourselves better, we can manage our emotions and protect our portfolios from their effects. This is especially critical if you are married or in a relationship that involves more than one personality in the decision-making process.

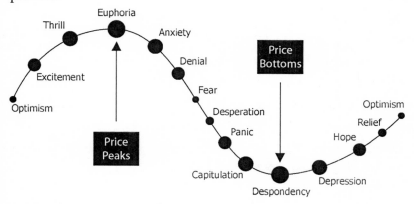

Figure 4.1   Cycle of emotions
Created from information presented by John Nofsinger on the Psychology Today website, July 15, 2008

---

22. Peter Bernstein, *Against the Gods: The Remarkable Story of Risk* (New York: Wiley, 1998).

As the Cycle of Emotions in figure 4.1 indicates, feelings move with the market in surprisingly predictable patterns. As prices move up, emotions gather speed until they peak at euphoria. But inevitably prices move down again, and investor emotions move down in tandem. Like all cycles, the Cycle of Emotions repeats itself over and over.

Classical economics teaches that people almost always act rationally, in their own best interest. On the classical economic view, markets are relatively stable and predictable, because it is easy to guess what rational people will do with their money. But despite what your college economics professor might have told you, people in an economy do not always act rationally.

In fact, investors regularly make decisions that drastically reduce their potential profits. According to the March 2011 DALBAR QAIB report, "equity and fixed income investors have underperformed the broad indices over the 20 years ending in 2010."[23] Most investors don't beat the market, and many end up performing significantly worse. The same report noted that the average investor "generally abandons investments at opportune times, often in response to bad news."[24] As the report indicated, average returns for equity mutual fund investors over the period of 1991 to 2010 were 3.83 percent. Compare this to the 9.14 percent return posted by the market over the same time period.

---

23. DALBAR, Inc. Research & Communications Division, "2011 QAIB: Quantitative Analysis of Investor Behavior," available for purchase from www.qaib.com, 3.
24. Ibid., 5.

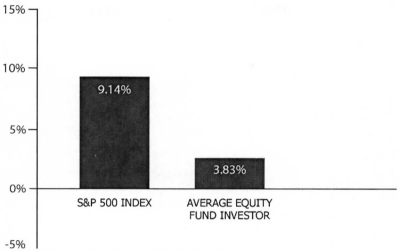

Figure 4.2 **Average annual returns**
Created from information presented by The Vanguard Group

Behavioral Finance Mentalities

Why do investors continually underperform compared to market benchmarks? Why do investors react so irrationally to bad news? The shift in our understanding of how people work began in the mid-twentieth century, and this shift affected classical economic beliefs. Psychology at this time had been focused on behavioral models of the person. Behaviorism suggested that everything people do is a result of the environment in which they find themselves. In the nature versus nurture debate, behaviorism fell wholly on the side of nurture. But as brain imaging became more prominent and our knowledge about the brain grew, cognitive models of the person gained more support. This was the nature side of the debate—rather than assuming that people acted the way they did because of their surroundings, cognitive theories suggested that our brains are hard-wired to encourage certain actions and responses, that we are born already possessing very specific characteristics.

New tools for explaining key deviations from rational decision-making began to arise from these cognitive theories. One of the first combinations of economic principles and these developments in cognitive psychology was Daniel Kahneman and Amos Tversky's 1979 work in prospect theory. Kahneman and Tversky's theory proposed that people are more risk-averse when potential profits are at stake, and are more risk-seeking when weighing potential losses.

For instance, they asked participants of a study in one case to imagine the following scenario: You receive $1,000, and then you have to choose between a 50 percent chance of receiving $1,000 more, or taking a guaranteed $500. Most people in the study chose the second option. But participants were then asked to imagine a slightly different scenario: You receive $1,000, but this time you have to choose between a 50 percent loss of $1,000 and a guaranteed loss of $500. Most people chose the first option.[25] Though the probable profitability was the same in both examples, participants were more risk-averse in the first scenario and more risk-seeking in the second scenario. Apparently, losing money feels worse than gaining money feels good.

We are in constant search for patterns to achieve greater success, but more importantly reduce our risk. Research by Duke University neuroscientists Scott Huettel, Peter Mack, and

25. Daniel Kahneman and Amos Tversky, "Prospect Theory: An Analysis of Decision under Risk," *Econometrica* 47, no. 2 (March 1979): 263–92.

Gregory McCarthy reveals that it takes only two similar events for the brain to expect that event to occur again.[26] This evidence suggest that it would take only two years of strong performance from a mutual fund for a typical investor to assume that the fund will continue to performance at its current rate or better. This explains why investors constantly are chasing hot funds with the belief that the managers' skills will not disappoint.

As behavioral finance exploded in the late twentieth century and early twenty-first century, other previously unexplainable actions became clear. Markets, made up as they are of individual people, are not perfect. Investors deviate from rational financial strategies in predictable, but perhaps unavoidable, directions. The following behavioral finance mentalities are just a few of the identified traps that investors can fall into. It is important for you to read the following with a critical eye, not at the content, but at you. Ask yourself, "Which of these categories might I find myself in?" You need to identify your strengths and weaknesses, so that you can work on them. If you are married or have a partner with whom you share financial decisions, this could not be more important. You need to know not just your biases but your partner's biases as well when it comes to making financial decisions. Think of it as a way to help keep each other accountable, so that you never have to say to each other, "I told you so, and if you would have listened to me we never would have made this decision."

Everyone follows one or more of these behavioral patterns when it comes to their investment decisions. Identifying your

---

26. Scott Huettel, Peter Mack, and Gregory McCarthy, "Perceiving Patterns in Random Series: Dynamic Processing of Sequence In Prefrontal Cortex," *Nature Neuroscience* 5, no. 5 (2002): 485–90.

own investing fallacies will be one of the most important steps you take to becoming a better investor. The saying that it starts with you . . . Well it's true, so let get to know you more.

Anchoring

How much does a loaf of bread cost? A bicycle? A car? What would you pay for a new house? These are your anchoring prices. Whether you are at the grocery store, on the housing market, or in the midst of stock trading, you operate with subconsciously anchored prices, and these are not always logically moored.

In an oft-cited study by Kahneman and Tversky, participants were asked to spin a wheel and then estimate whether the percentage of the U.N. made up of African countries was higher or lower than the number on which they had landed.[27] Afterward, the same participants were asked to give an actual estimate. Their answers varied wildly depending on the number they had spun—those who had spun 10 estimated on average that 25 percent of the U.N. was African, while those who had spun 60 estimated around 45 percent.

The roulette number acted as an anchor, a point of reference that significantly influenced the estimates of the participants, even if it did not have direct bearing on the subject at hand. This tendency to anchor values plays a major role in investor bias. In an investing scenario, an investor might see a stock priced one day at $50 rise to $65 the next. Believing the stock is overvalued because he has anchored the price at $50, the investor refuses to purchase what turns out to be a rapidly rising stock that ultimately would have been profitable.

---

27. Daniel Kahneman and Amos Tversky, "Judgment under Uncertainty: Heuristics and Biases," *Science* 185 (1974): 1124–31.

Anchoring is inevitable, and no matter how hard you try to avoid it, you are going to anchor prices. While this can sometimes work in your favor, like when you know you can find toothpaste cheaper at Target so you pass it by in Vons, it can also hinder you. Anchored values can quickly become obsolete as markets shift. If you want to invest successfully, you have to take into account the effect that anchoring has on the individual investor's market decisions.

Gambler's Fallacy

Imagine you are flipping a coin. If the coin lands on heads five times in a row, are the chances that the coin will land on tails higher the next time you flip it? The average person is inclined to say yes. But in reality, the coin is no more likely to land on tails the sixth time you flip it. The 50-50 chance of a coin toss is never dependent on the results of previous flips.

While classical economic models assume that the individual investor operates with a rational understanding of probability, scenarios such as coin flips indicate that most investors, in fact, don't. The fallacy of the gambler is to believe that a given result is due—that the coin "has" to land on tails if it has landed on heads for multiple tosses in a row, or that a stock value "has" to go up if it has fallen for several consecutive days or weeks.

Investors, unfortunately, tend to act much like conventional gamblers. In an extended discussion that builds upon Kahneman and Tversky's prospect theory, Nicholas Barberis describes the typical trajectory of a gambler's trip to a casino. The gambler, before entering the casino, plans to keep gambling only if he is winning. If he is losing, he plans to stop and cut his losses. Once he enters the casino and begins to play, however, the gambler does exactly the opposite: He keeps gambling if he is losing, and he stops gambling if he wins a significant amount.[28] Barberis extends this image to the typical investor:

> We find that, when the naive trader buys the stock at time 0 [the beginning of the study], his initial plan parallels that of the naive gambler: he plans to keep holding the stock if its price remains above purchase price, but to sell it if its price falls below purchase price. His actual selling behavior, however, follows the opposite pattern: he holds on to the stock if it falls below purchase price but sells it if it rises significantly above purchase price.[29]

Like any gambler, you might have the best of intentions before you step into the casino, or into the stock market. But over and over, investors prove that the gambler's fallacy is hard to escape. While it might seem like you have to sell that stock because it is impossible for it to continue rising, the opposite could in fact be the truth, and you could be substantially selling yourself short. In the same manner, you might believe that this losing stock just has to turn around at some point, but you could very well be holding on to a toxic asset that will upset your portfolio.

Conformity and Herding

Sometimes it pays to fit in. After all, human infants begin imitating the facial expressions of those around them just hours after birth, and this imitative behavior assists in cognitive and

---

28. Nicholas Barberis, "A Model of Casino Gambling" (paper presented at the Yale Workshop in Behavioral Finance, March 2009): 4.
29. Ibid., 31.

social development.[30] But when it comes to investment strategies, imitation is at best neutral, and at worst a seriously negative influence on a portfolio's profitability. You've seen this dynamic at work: Every bubble and bust in an economic cycle is, on some level, the result of herd behavior. While a single individual might not have priced her house in 2006 at nearly two times its 2005 value, the actions of a herd of people scrambling to buy houses (with subprime mortgages, no less) inflated prices and set the stage for the 2007 crash.

The herding behavior of investors, a well-documented phenomenon, can wreak havoc with a single company's stock or with the entire market. In "Herd Behavior in Financial Markets," Sushil Bikhchandani and Sunil Sharma offer a hypothetical scenario to depict the effects of investor herding. In a group of 100 investors with disparate assets and investment needs, 20 are optimistic about an emerging market and decide to invest in it. Some of the remaining 80 decide to jump on the bandwagon, and soon most of the 100 investors commit to this emerging market. In this sort of situation, "investors who decide early may be crucial in determining which way the majority will decide[,] . . . the decision that investors herd on may well be incorrect," and if new information arises after a bad decision, "they are likely to eventually reverse their decision, starting a herd in the opposite direction. This, in turn, increases volatility in the market."[31] The impulse to conform

---

30. Sushil Bikhchandani, David Hirshleifer, and Ivo Welc, "Learning from the Behavior of Others: Conformity, Fads, and Informational Cascades," *Journal of Economic Perspectives* 12, no. 3 (1998): 151–70.
31. Sushil Bikhchandani and Sunil Sharma, "Herd Behavior in Financial Markets," *IMF Staff Papers* 47, no. 3 (2001): 280–81.

drives market instability and decreases long-term profitability.

If your investment strategies are directed by the latest, greatest investment trend, your assets are going to rise and fall with the inevitable bursting bubble that is sure to follow. And your hedge fund manager is not immune to this dynamic. In fact, a manager has little to lose in following the crowd. If a trendy investment pays off, the manager makes money and avoids the wrath of clients who might otherwise blame her for missing out on a major opportunity. If the investment trend turns out to be a giant bust, the manager can point to her colleagues and observe that they were all mistaken. Unfortunately, this approach neglects to acknowledge an often-ignored truth: Just because everyone is doing it, that doesn't make it right. Or profitable, for that matter.

Mental Accounting

Losing money hurts. In fact, losing money feels significantly worse than gaining money feels good, a concept often described as "loss aversion." Humans, averse to pain as we are, try to minimize the sting of financial losses and maximize the perception of financial gains through mental accounting. Mental accounting can take many forms. Imagine a person who decides to divide all of his expenses into a predetermined budget. At the end of the month, he realizes he hasn't spent all of the money in his gas budget, so he goes to the movies and orders the largest popcorn and soda he can find, guilt-free. In a similar manner, a grocery shopper, upon seeing bananas are half off, buys twice as many for the same amount she normally spends on bananas. Some of those bananas go bad and she has to throw them out, but she doesn't mind because she feels like she didn't really spend anything on them. These hypothetical spenders are not treating money like it is fungible, and this is a major investment mistake.

Fungible items are interchangeable, and money might be the most fungible thing there is. Money that was earmarked to fill up your car is still money, and spending those extra funds on a frivolous evening for no other reason is no different than paying straight out of your checking account. Further, purchasing goods that you wouldn't have bought otherwise, merely because they are on sale, does not save you money— in fact, you have in a very real sense lost the money that you needlessly spent. Richard Thaler offers a common mental accounting blunder, in which an investor who needs to liquidate some of his assets sells a profitable stock and retains a losing one because of the pain of realizing the paper losses of the unprofitable stock. While a "rational investor will choose to sell the loser because capital gains are taxable and capital losses are deductible," research shows that "investors were more likely to sell one of their stocks that had increased in value than one of their stocks that had decreased."[32]

Thaler further describes studies in which investors, shown year-by-year returns of stocks and bonds, chose to invest in bonds. Investors shown returns from stocks and bonds over a thirty-year period, however, chose to invest in stocks.[33] Sometimes the best choice for the long term isn't obvious. Mental accounting, and the loss aversion that goes along with it, can easily get in the way of your portfolio's profitability.

32. Richard H. Thaler, "Mental Accounting Matters," *Journal of Behavioral Decision Making* 12 (1999): 189.
33. Thaler, "Mental Accounting," 200.

Overconfidence

Are you a good driver? Are you a better-than-average driver? Studies have shown that there is a 93 percent chance that you will respond "yes" to these questions.[34] Of course, 93 percent of drivers cannot be above average—by definition, only 50 percent of any given group can be above average. And yet, we persist in thinking that we are. In another study, engineers were asked to rank themselves according to their performance in a particular firm: 37 percent of them ranked themselves in the top 5 percent.[35] Where does this huge disconnect between reality and self-perception occur?

According to an analysis by Don Moore and Paul Healy, psychologists have identified three main strains of overconfidence. *Overestimation* includes the impulse to overstate or predict inaccurately one's abilities, such as performance on a test or length of time required to complete a task. *Overplacement* describes the tendency to consider oneself above average in a range of categories. *Overprecision* involves an unmerited assurance in one's guesses or beliefs.[36]

From an investment standpoint, these psychological traits can cause of lot of harm. The overestimating investor might significantly overshoot his ability to choose profitable stocks and end up with a portfolio of underperforming assets that he desperately retains in an attempt to validate his original (and

---

34. Ola Svenson, "Are We All Less Risky and More Skillful than our Fellow Drivers?" *Acta Psychologica* 47, no. 2 (1981): 143–48.
35. Todd R. Zenger, "Why Do Employers Only Reward Extreme Performance? Examining the Relationships among Performance, Pay, and Turnover," *Administrative Science Quarterly* 37 (1992): 198–219.
36. Don Moore and Paul J. Healy, "The Trouble with Overconfidence," *Psychological Review* 115, no. 2 (2008): 502–17.

very inaccurate) perception of himself. The overplacing investor who assumes she is better than average, especially if she is a fund manager, might find a rude awakening when she jumps into a rapidly devaluing market at the wrong time. The overprecise investor, believing that his last few trades prove his superior ability to choose the perfect times to buy and sell, begins trading excessively and swiftly eliminates his profits.

Overconfidence in the market on a macro level has been linked to the formation of bubbles and their resulting constrictions. When investors are convinced that their information regarding a given market is more accurate than it actually is, speculation proliferates, and prices rapidly outpace market values. Agents assuming that other investors are more optimistic about a given market "pay prices that exceed their own valuation of future dividends, because they believe that in the future they will find a buyer willing to pay even more."[37] Such overconfidence on the part of both the buyers and the sellers leads to volatility, inaccurate prices, and larger crashes.

Overreactions and the Availability Heuristic

Connected in many ways to investor overconfidence, market overreactions are a major factor in the short-term volatility of the market. When new information about a given stock or company is released, markets often over- or underreact, causing short-term misvaluations. Indeed, the tendency to overreact to news is a well-documented psychological occurrence. In the classic article "Does the Stock Market Overreact?" Werner F.M. De Bondt and Richard Thaler, citing the litany of studies

---

37. José Scheinkman and Wei Xiong, "Overconfidence and Speculative Bubbles," *Journal of Political Economy* 11, no. 6 (2003): 1183–1219.

that establish the propensity to overreact to new information, examine the effects of news on the stock market. By tracking the highest- and lowest-performing stocks over a three-year period, De Bondt and Thaler discovered that the low-end stocks consistently beat the market index, while the high-end stocks struggled.[38] It seems investors reacted too positively to good news about the high-performing stocks, and so initial overvaluations were later corrected, causing the stock to fall. Low-performing stocks, on the other hand, fell too precipitously after bad news, causing them to become undervalued and subsequently fostering long-term growth.

The frequency with which investors encounter the name of a given stock, the level of recognition a stock has, and how recent new information about a stock is all factor into decisions made through the availability heuristic. A heuristic is a lens or interpretive model through which individuals process information and decision-making. The availability heuristic is a cognitive model of sorts that influences perceptions based on ease of recall and immediate familiarity. A quick example: In the English language, does the letter r occur more frequently at the beginning of a word, or as the third letter of a word? This was a question posed by researchers in a study cited by Kahneman and Tversky.[39] Most participants said r is most often found at the beginning of words. This, however, is not the case—you are much more likely to encounter the letter r as the third letter of an English word. The study concluded that participants could recall words that began with r much more easily than

38. Werner F.M. De Bondt and Richard Thaler, "Does the Stock Market Overreact?" *The Journal of Finance* 40, no. 3 (1985): 793–805.
39. Kahneman and Tversky, "Judgment under Uncertainty," 1127.

they could words that had r as their third letter because it is easier to remember words in an alphabetized fashion.

Operating according to the availability heuristic can lead to poor investment decisions, especially when it comes to acting according to new information on the stock market. An investor can overlook an investment opportunity simply because it is unfamiliar and not called to mind easily, making it seem like an undesirable choice. Likewise, an investor can latch on to a stock merely because it has been mentioned recently in the media and so its familiarity makes it seem like a good idea. Between the availability heuristic and the tendency to overreaction, investing based on financial news and new information can be quite tricky. It is not a strategy for the faint of heart, or the desirous of strong returns.

Confirmation and Hindsight Bias

As if the intertwined influences of overconfidence, overreactions, and the availability heuristic were not enough, another set of biases regularly plagues investors. Confirmation bias, the tendency for individuals to seek out supportive evidence for what they already think is true, leads investors to avoid potentially negative information. Hindsight bias, the propensity to view past events as if they were predictable—as if one knew all along that they were going to occur—feeds into the overconfidence loop and reduces investor performance. The combination of these biases can be financially toxic.

Confirmation bias infiltrates many areas of our lives. It's the mechanism behind both psychics and placebos: Someone who wants to believe that the palm reading he just received was from a real fortune teller will see every new acquaintance as a "tall, mysterious stranger" and treat every piece of mail like a "package destined to create new and exciting opportunities." Likewise, someone who has been given an innocuous pill to alleviate her cold symptoms will tend to interpret any reprieve as a result of the "medicine" she took. But confirmation bias's effects are especially pronounced when it comes to investments. In an analysis of stock market message boards, researchers found that investors posting messages exhibited marked biases about their trading decisions. The stronger the confirmation bias investors displayed, the higher their rates of overconfidence were. This overconfidence led to more frequent trading and lower overall returns.[40] By paying attention to an echo chamber of opinions they already held, the investors ignored or avoided information to the contrary, effectually ensuring themselves reduced long-term profitability.

Hindsight bias runs rampant in the wake of major financial catastrophes, but it arises in less visible contexts as well. You can see it firsthand after every market crash—commentators and water-cooler philosophers alike will be glad to let you know that they saw it coming. But this bias is more insidious in its effects on the day-to-day volatility of investments. In an examination of investment bankers in Frankfurt and London, researchers found that the bankers with the lowest levels of hindsight bias had the highest investment returns. Not a single banker with high levels of hindsight bias had high earnings.[41]

40. JaeHong Park, Prabhudev Konana, Bin Gu, Alok Kumar, and Rajagopal Raghunathan, "Confirmation Bias, Overconfidence, and Investment Performance: Evidence from Stock Message Boards" (McCombs Research Paper Series No. IROM-07-10, July 12, 2010).
41. Bruno Biais and Martin Weber, "Hindsight Bias, Risk Perception and Investment Performance," *Management Science* 55, no. 6 (June 2009): 1018–29.

Hindsight bias was found to be an impediment to learning and a factor in ultimately harmful overconfidence.

Anchoring, gambler's fallacy, conformity and herding, mental accounting, overconfidence, overreactions and the availability heuristic, confirmation and hindsight bias—these are just a few of the natural tendencies waging war with your long-term profitability. But this is just what is happening on the outside. As investors, we have a host of internal obstacles to effective investing as well. Our brains simply were not designed for Wall Street, a truth that the field of neurofinance makes all too clear.

> *Neurofinance: What Goes on in Your Head Controls What Goes on in Your Portfolio*

Neurofinance

When it comes to investing, self-knowledge is more important than intelligence. Your brain-based, cognitive reactions to investment decisions will affect your long-term portfolio performance far more than any amount of factual knowledge you can collect. The field of neurofinance makes this clear. Neurofinance, the application of neuroscience to the marketplace, seeks to understand why and how individual financial decisions are made, by studying the brain. While behavioral finance examines observed behavior, neurofinance looks at what is going on underneath the surface—quite literally.

The conclusions drawn from neurofinancial data have far-ranging applications. By looking at the areas of brain that are activated when fear and greed exist, we can understand the source of some of our most seemingly irrational investment behavior. For instance, fear dominates reason and accounts for excessive risk aversion in many cases. Greed also distorts reason. Thanks to neuroscientists, we can pinpoint the exact spots in the brain where fear and greed arise. This sort of knowledge is incredibly empowering. An understanding of neurofinance provides you as an individual investor with an advantage, because you can understand on a deeper level the need for tools of self-knowledge and self-discipline. You might not be able to control your emotions completely, but you can work around them once you understand how your brain functions. What could be more important than knowing what is going on inside your head?

According to *Financial Times's* John Authers, investors must find a balance between greed and fear if they are going to grow their investments successfully. We can find this balance only by gaining a thorough understanding of how our brains function to create these emotions. Authers references education theorist Howard Gardner's multiple intelligences—logical-mathematical, verbal-linguistic, spatial-mechanical, musical, bodily, interpersonal, and intrapersonal—and argues that "this last, self-knowledge, may be more important for investing than logical intelligence."[42]

---

42. John Authers, "Investing Insights that Get Inside Your Head," *Financial Times*, December 8, 2006, accessed September 20, 2011, http://www.ft.com/cms/s/0/f8e0cb58-86b7-11db-9ad5-0000779e2340.html#axzz1YWAF3cKw

Consider figure 4.3:

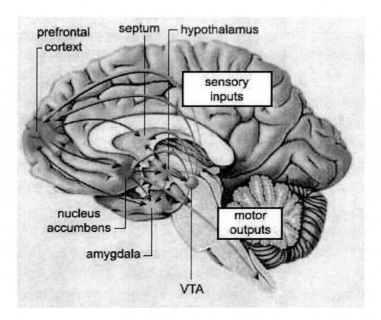

Figure 4.3   Location of the nucleus accumbens in the human brain
Retrieved from http://neurtronics.webs.com/aboutthenucleusaccumb.htm

This diagram might look complicated, but it represents astounding research that has located one of the sources of human emotions ranging from pleasure to fear: the nucleus accumbens. In an early study that tested this area in the brains of rats, the rats preferred to press a lever that stimulated the nucleus accumbens more than eating or drinking—it feels that good.[43] This is where dopamine is released, and it is a key link in the pleasure circuit of the brain. Too much stimulation, and

---

43. Neurtronicsweb, "About the Nucleus Accumbens,"accessed December 20, 2011, http://neurtronics.webs.com/aboutthenucleusaccumb.htm

addictions and dependencies can quickly form. Anything that stimulates this part of the brain—alcohol, drugs, food, gambling—triggers dopamine release and creates a pleasurable association with the stimulant, causing a desire for more. The process repeats itself, and the cravings can easily escalate to dangerous levels.

Such a stimulus-pleasure link has wide application in our daily lives, but its connection to financial decisions is especially apt. Behind every successful stock trade is a dopamine release. The more a person trades, the greater the impulse to trade becomes. The risks multiply to meet the growing need for greater payoff, and the cycle can soon spiral to alarming heights. From a neurological perspective, greed is no mystery.

In a similar fashion, the anterior insula governs the mechanisms of fear. Neuroscientists Camelia M. Kuhnen and Brian Knutson conducted a study to compare the different functions of the nucleus accumbens and the anterior insula. Study participants played an investment simulation game while their brains

> *"There is a foolish corner in the brain of the wisest man."*
> —Aristotle 384 B.C.-322 B.C.

were monitored through MRI. Kuhnen and Knutson found that risk-seeking behavior was associated with activity in the nucleus accumbens, while risk-averse behavior correlated with activity in the anterior insula.[44] When participants had lost a significant amount of funds, they began to choose bonds over stocks, even when this was not the rational choice, and

---

44. Camelia M. Kuhnen and Brian Knutson, "The Neural Basis of Financial Risk-Taking," *Neuron* 47 (2005): 763–70.

the activation of the anterior insula reflected this. Likewise, participants with a winning streak tended to choose riskier options, as the nucleus accumbens prodded them to keep seeking that dopamine high.

In a recent NPR interview, Kuhnen explained how just hearing bad news can activate that anterior insula and make investors more risk-averse, even when it isn't the most rational investment choice. "When we're presented news in this very emotional way, very bombastic way, it's in our nature to pay more attention to it," Kuhnen said. "I'm trying to tell people to just chill out. They should calm down. They should really just sit down and understand what is new today."[45] In the same interview, Kuhnen's fellow professor Adam Galinsky offered an illustration to show why we have that risk-averse reaction in the first place. According to Galinsky, it probably worked well for our ancestors thousands of years ago. People in hunter-gatherer societies needed to follow the herd for basic survival—if there was a tiger on the prowl, it was in your best interest to panic and run at the first mention of a predator nearby, avoiding any possible risk as quickly as possible.[46]

But news doesn't work quite the same way today. If you hear potentially alarming investment news, you're much better off taking the time to sit down and think about the situation without immediately allowing your natural emotional response to dictate your actions. You might not be able to control your

---

45. Quoted in Sonari Glinton, "How Does Financial News Affect Your Brain?" NPR (August 16, 2011), accessed September 21, 2011, http://www.npr.org/2011/08/16/139680650/how-does-market-coverage-impact-your-brain

46. Ibid.

emotions, but you can work with them to ensure your assets are protected from your own impulses for self-protection.

In another study, researchers actually stimulated parts of the brain that control decision-making, to affect participants' risk-taking behaviors.[47] The study subjects were divided into test and control groups (though all participants were told that their brains were being stimulated, to make sure the results would not be skewed). Researchers increased stimulation of the right side of the dorsolateral prefrontal cortex and decreased stimulation of the left side in the brains of the test group to assess the effects of this sort of brain activity.

To test participants' willingness to take risks, researchers gave them a series of choices, and told them to try to gain as many points as they could. The experiment worked like this: You are given six boxes, and one of the boxes has a token inside of it. The boxes are a mix of pink and blue, and you have to choose which color you think has the token. But every round is different—sometimes there are five blue boxes and one pink box; sometimes there are three blue boxes and three pink boxes, and so on. If you pick the right color, you gain points, but if you pick the wrong color, you lose points. Obviously, if there are five pink boxes and one blue box, the coin is more likely to be in a pink box. But you get more points if you choose the blue box and it happens to have the token inside, because the more risky the choice, the greater the payoff, just as if you are betting on horses at a racetrack.

---

47. Shirley Fecteau, Daria Knoch, Felipe Fregni, Natasha Sultani, Paulo Boggio, and Alvaro Pascual-Leon, "Diminishing Risk-Taking Behavior by Modulating Activity in the Prefrontal Cortex: A Direct Current Stimulation Study," *The Journal of Neuroscience* 27(46): 12,500–05.

People in the study who were receiving the brain stimulation overwhelmingly chose the least risky options, regardless
of the potential reward (if there were five pink boxes and one
blue box, they would always choose pink, even if choosing blue
meant they could possibly win big). Activity in a particular
part of their brains made them less likely to make risky decisions. As it turns out, very specific brain stimulation can in fact
make people more risk-averse. We are more manipulable than
we think.

Our feelings have a great deal to do with the extent to which
we can be manipulated. While our feelings are essential to what
we would consider rational decision-making, they can just as
easily lead us astray. This is an important distinction to make.
Emotions are not all bad. As scientists have found, we need
emotions to act rationally, in our own best interest.

Consider, for example, a study that illustrates how important
feelings are to healthy brain functioning. Antonio Damasio, in
his book *Descartes' Error*, describes an experiment in which the
responses of normal adults were compared to those of people
with frontal lobe damage.[48] All participants were asked to play
a gambling game: Each person was given $2,000 (fake money,
but it looked real) and told to sit down before a card dealer with
four stacks of cards—A, B, C, and D. The card dealer told the
people in the study to choose a card to flip over, and if it had a
monetary gain written on it, the participant would receive that
much. If the card had a loss, the person had to pay the written
amount out of the money they were given.

---

48. Antonio Damasio, *Descartes' Error* (New York: Grosset/Putnam, 1994),
212–17.

The participants were unaware that stacks A and B contained large gains but also large losses, meaning they would eventually come out in the hole if they consistently chose A or B cards. Stacks C and D, however, contained smaller gains but also significantly smaller losses, and consistently choosing these cards would lead to a net gain. Normal subjects began with random card choices, but they quickly formed a "hunch" that A and B were "dangerous," and so they eventually favored C and D cards.[49]

Participants with frontal lobe damage, however, began choosing randomly but ended up favoring the A and B cards, even though most of them lost so much money, they had to ask for a loan halfway through the experimental game. It seems that an intact frontal lobe in the normal participants allowed their brains to subconsciously develop a feeling about which cards were "good" and which were "bad," ultimately causing them to act in a rational manner. Participants whose brains had lost the ability to create that feeling could otherwise function normally, but their ability to sense, to *feel* the outcome of a scenario was severely impaired.

To this extent, then, it is apparent that feelings are inescapably a part of rational decision-making. Take away feelings, and you take away the brain's capacity for forming patterns and predicting possible outcomes. But feelings, like so much else, are a double-edged sword.

In yet another study, participants were monitored by MRI as they played a gambling game in which they had to choose between two colors in a random wheel spin. They were shown the result of the option they didn't choose each time, which was

---

49. Ibid., 213.

meant to give them a feeling of regret. Researchers found that participants became increasingly risk-averse as the simulation progressed. The more regret that participants registered on the MRI, the more likely they were to avoid risky decisions in the simulation.[50] In this case, the feelings generated by their brains induced behavior that ultimately led to less overall profit for them. They were simply unable to act in their own best interest.

Summary

So what does this all mean? It means that when you hear bad financial news, your brain is going to tell you to panic and sell. It means that when you make a few good trades, your brain is likely going to push you toward riskier and riskier deals to keep that good feeling going. It means that we as humans are easily manipulated by our environment. We don't live on the savanna anymore. The fear that kept us away from predators and the greed that compelled us to stockpile resources were once survival skills. Now, they're enemies to our financial well-being. Breaking this rule and acknowledging that you cannot control your emotions, while knowing **you can manage them through self-awareness, is vital.**

50. Giorgio Coricelli, Hugo D. Critchley, Mateus Joffily, John P. O'Doherty, Angela Sirigu, and Raymond J. Dolan, "Regret and Its Avoidance: A Neuroimaging Study of Choice Behavior," *Nature Neuroscience* 8, no. 9 (September 2005): 1255–62, accessed September 22, 2011, doi:10.1038/nn1514

5.

Take Action

"Action expresses priorities."
Mohandas K. Gandhi

This chapter is about taking what you have learned and putting it into action. I have laid out the steps you need to take to break the rules, efficiently and effectively. As you set out to implement your plan, you will need to decide if you want to manage all aspects of the investment and planning process or if you would prefer to hire a financial advisor. If you want to hire an advisor, read the "Hiring a Financial Advisor" section to make sure you are selecting the right person to help guide your financial future. Finding the right one is just not as simple as googling your local Fidelity or Merrill Lynch office. In fact, that may be the last place you want to find your advisor.

TAKE ACTION FORMULA

Gather → Reflect → Plan → Implement → Revisit

STEP 1: GATHER

I. Know Your Destination

<u>Goals & Values:</u> Answer the following questions, taken from Chapter 1. If you are married or have a partner, you need to answer these separately as well as together to ensure you have a plan that both of you can stick to.

Questions to Ask Yourself and Your Family

1. Where are you today?
2. Where do you want to be in the future?
3. How will you get there?
4. What is important about money to you?
5. What does financial success look like to you?
6. What does financial failure look like to you?
7. What do you want for your children? Your parents? Other family members?
8. What impact do you want to have in your community?
9. When you think about your money, what specific concerns, needs, or feelings come to mind?
10. How do you want to be remembered and/or what is the legacy that you want to leave?

Once you have this information, do not rush, but take the time to reflect and engage in conversation about what you have learned about yourself and your partner. This should be your foundation as you move forward to build a portfolio for your future.

II. Know Your Situation

Current/Future Resources: This step is about looking at your current job or income sources and assets. This is where a list of assets and liabilities comes into account.

You will want to also address some practical questions as well:

1. What is your time horizon?
2. What are your liquidity needs?
3. What is your personal risk tolerance?
4. How much risk can you "AFFORD" to take?
5. What are your income needs?

Advisor or No Advisor: Whether you currently have an advisor or not, you should consider the elements of choosing an advisor carefully. Below are some questions that can help you determine your investment advisory needs:

1. How involved do I want to be in the investing process?
2. How qualified am I to make sure the plan is properly constructed?
3. Do I have the time to constantly ensure my plan is on target?
4. Do I need help staying focused and unemotional when markets move up and down?

III. Know Yourself

Emotional Strengths and Weaknesses: It is so critical for you to take your time here. Again, if you are married or have a partner, you want to find out what his or her emotional tendencies are when making a financial decision. Once these are identified, share this information and keep it handy as you walk through the rest of the steps.

At this point, it may be helpful for you to complete an emotional intelligence assessment, to give you a better understanding of your own emotional strengths and weaknesses. One such assessment is available from TalentSmart, at:

http://www.talentsmart.com/products/surveys.php

The TalentSmart Emotional Intelligence Appraisal will give you a measure of your EQ and allow you to reflect on how your tendencies and reactions affect all areas of your life.

IV. Know Your Options

Passive vs. Active Investing: In Chapter 2, we discussed at length the challenges that active investors face in trying to beat the market. You need to understand the difference between passive and active investing, because whether you manage your money personally or hire an advisor, you are going to need to make crucial decisions in this area.

V. Know Your Environment

Bull and Bear Secular Markets: As you discover more about the type of investment philosophy you desire for your portfolio, you must also pay attention to the macro elements that are surrounding these decisions. Again, whether you are doing it yourself or hiring an advisor, knowing the potential headwinds or tailwinds is important to how you approach your asset allocation.

STEP 2: REFLECT

When I think of reflecting, the word "listen" always comes to mind. I want to you to reflect on all that you have gathered and listen to what your responses are saying to you and your spouse/partner. Analyze it under all possible circumstances that you want to happen, as well as the ones that you may not want to see take place. What happens if there is a job loss, or someone passes away? This process is so important, because you will be building a solid foundation for what your financial path is to look like and what it is not to look like. You will be empowered to keep it on track when the emotional storms come and try to take it off course. As you reflect, begin to write down your thoughts and compare those to your original answers to see how they are being molded into the core of what you want for your plan.

STEP 3: PLAN

I recommend that you find a financial planner who has advanced tools that can help you analyze the information you have in a cohesive plan (see "How to Hire a Financial Advisor" at the end of this chapter for more details). A good plan takes into account all of the information that you have personally gathered, but then it looks at other important elements that may affect the end results. The big one is inflation. This is critical to understand and forecast what it may be during the time frames that you are looking at. Also, you want to see what taxes and market loss may do to the impact of the plan. A good plan must be able to stress test multiple outcomes and scenarios before being implemented.

> *"The great end of life is not knowledge but action."*
> —*Thomas Henry Huxley, 1887*

STEP 4: IMPLEMENT

After you have a plan, you need to take action. It is the details that will be crucial to the effective implementation of your plan. Ensure that you have the following elements in place:

1. IPS (Investment Policy Statement)
2. The asset allocation strategy
3. Tax strategy
4. Cost of portfolio
5. Follow plan

STEP 5: REVISIT

Have a follow-up plan to measure whether your portfolio is on track to hit the projections that you have set. This is straightforward, but it needs to be a part of the overall financial strategy. One of the big reasons that you must revisit your plan is because when you hit the "go" button, be rest assured that life has a way of changing. Making sure that your portfolio is being flexible to winds of change is important. Also, by sitting down and revisiting your plan, you are strengthening your understanding of your path, and this helps build the emotion muscles that you need as an investor.

Hiring a Financial Advisor

Disclosure: It is important for you to know that I am an independent registered investment advisor, so I am biased toward seeking advice from someone who operates in this manner.

> *A smart man makes a mistake, learns from it, and never makes that mistake again. But a wise man finds a smart man and learns from him how to avoid the mistake altogether.*
> *—Roy H. Williams*

If you find the right financial planner, it can make your investment process easier and more enjoyable. A good advisor can bring more time for you, discipline during turbulent markets, access to top strategies, and intelligence to your portfolio. A bad advisor can simply do the opposite of what I just mentioned. I believe that a good advisor embodies two key elements that every investor deserves. The first is TRUST, and second is COMPETENCE. You must be able to trust your advisor, but they must also be competent to deliver. The following are simple but extremely important criteria you should use when working with an advisor. If you are currently working with one, use this information to see whether he or she fits, and if not, you may need to find someone else who will be on your side financially.

The most important question you want to ask your financial advisor is, "Do you have a fiduciary or a suitability responsibility to our relationship?" Maybe you are asking what is the difference and why would this be important.

The difference between fiduciary and suitability can be explained using this analogy that comes from Richard Ferri.[51] Let's say you walk into a Ford dealership. A salesperson working there is not going to try to sell you a vehicle that is suitable to meet your needs. The salesperson is not going to recommend a vehicle made by Toyota or any other competitor, even if that salesperson believes it would be a better fit for you. In contrast, what if you personally hired a car-buying consultant to help you select a vehicle? This consultant would be obligated to recommend the best vehicle for your needs, regardless of the make or model. The Ford salesperson is recommending something suitable that he or she can sell to you, but the car buying consultant is a fiduciary who is obligated to recommend the best vehicle.

One question to ask your financial advisor (and not to be shy about it) is "How do you get paid?" Every professional is going to be compensated for his or her time and advice, and you must know that in the financial industry there are several ways you

---

51. Richard A. Ferri, *The Power of Passive Investing: More Wealth with Less Work* (Hoboken, New Jersey: Wiley), 2011.

can be paid for your efforts. What you want is someone who is going to be paid a "fee," like a CPA, for services rendered, NOT "commissions" for selling you mutual funds or stocks. Below are my recommend criteria to use when looking to hire an advisor.

1. Advisor is Compensated Using a Fee-Based Structure

When you hire a fee-based advisor, you will pay a percentage of your portfolio's assets each year, as opposed to a commission on each transaction. As a result, a fee-based advisor's interests are aligned with yours. The advisor does well only if your portfolio is doing well. This structure motivates him/her to give the best advice at all times, and isn't that what we all want, especially when it comes to money?

Compare this to broker/dealers, who will earn commissions based upon their recommendation for the stocks and mutual funds in their plan. A commission-based advisor may be more likely to suggest that you make a lot of transactions in your portfolio, even if these are not in your best interest. Commissioned advisors get paid based on when you buy and sell, and the frequency behind that increases their compensation. There is an inherent conflict of interest in the commission-based approach to portfolio management.

2. Advisor is a Registered Investment Advisor (RIA)

In the financial world, there are many different titles people can carry to give the impression that they are there to give the best advice. It is important to know what lies beneath these titles and how they are going to deliver their services to you. A financial advisor falls under either the title of broker/dealer (a stockbroker) or registered investment advisor (RIA).

It is my professional opinion that you should work with someone who is an RIA. As a financial planner myself, I am a registered investment advisor, because I feel this is the best way to offer counsel to clients. RIAs have a fiduciary responsibility to provide their clients with the highest possible standard of care. As a fiduciary, an RIA is required by law to look out for the investor's best interest and to completely and objectively disclose all important information in his or her dealings. This information can be found in a document know as Form ADV, which clearly outlines the services offered, compensation, and any other outside businesses relationship that may be involved. You can find this at www.adviserinfo.sec.gov.

The opposite is true for broker/dealers, who are not currently held to the same standards. They are not legally required to always work in your best interest, and this may create a conflict of interest at times. Also, it is difficult for an investor to see all of the costs associated with this sort of business relationship at the outset, so be aware of the potential financial burden.

3. Advisor is Independent

There are many great brands out there in the investment world that you may have come to know over the years. Even banks have been getting into the advisory business by offering "private group" status. But I want to give you a sense of caution if you go and sit down in these offices. Just because you may be sitting with a fee-based advisor who works at a big shop, be careful. These advisors may have a bias toward their firm's proprietary products that you may not be aware of. This is why working with an independent RIA can benefit you, because

RIAs have no boss telling them how to structure their plans or to maximize profits to make shareholders happy. When you work with an independent RIA, you should be getting the best advice they can offer. You want the best advice at all times, and having a qualified independent RIA on your side can do that for you.

Interview Questions for a Potential Advisor

Compensation

- How do you get paid if we engage in a relationship?

Discovery Process

- How do you go about discovering and assessing my goals and objectives?
- How do my values fit inside your discovery process?
- How do you evaluate my tolerance for risk in building a portfolio?
- Do you prepare an Investment Policy Statement for your clients?

Asset Allocation

- What is your philosophy behind your approach to active vs. passive management in your clients' portfolios?
- Do you use a strategic or tactical asset-allocation strategy in your portfolios?

- How do bear and bull secular markets affect your asset allocation decisions?

Investments

- What types of investment vehicles do you offer to your clients and why?
- Do you tend to favor one type of investment vehicle over another, and why/why not?
- How do you determine which investments are the most suitable for my situation?
- What factors do you take into consideration when coming up with your recommendations on selecting specific investment vehicles?

Rebalancing and Reporting

- What is your rebalancing policy for your clients?
- Do you provide reports for your clients? How often do you send them out?

6.

Rule 5: In Me I Trust

I believe in Christianity as I believe that the sun has risen: not only because I see it, but because by it I see everything else."
C.S. Lewis

Have you ever had the feeling of something not being 100 percent complete? Well, that was the feeling I had about this book as we were making the final changes to the manuscript. This feeling was pressed upon my heart to write this last rule that we must all break on a daily basis. This is not just a rule, but also THE rule in order to achieve the true peace of mind that you desire. It's the universal truth behind not just financial happiness, but the meaning to your life and mine. The rule we need to follow is IN GOD WE TRUST, not in ME I trust. Maybe this statement offends you as you read it, or maybe you agree, or maybe you are not sure. Whatever you're feeling, I ask that you finish reading the rest of this chapter.

I'm not sure about you, but I struggle with this idea about breaking a rule that is about trusting me, because ultimately it comes down to me! Right? It's all about me? Especially when it comes to money, we love to make it about me, because isn't that the whole purpose? It's about working hard so that I can buy the dream house and dream car and all of what my heart desires.

I buy certain clothes, so others are impressed. I go to the gym to look good for others to notice. I like being in charge. I like winning. I like nice things. I like being successful. I like when people like me. I like it when I think I'm looking good. I like feeling healthy. I like the feeling of making a good decision, especially if it is one for financial gain. Maybe you are reading this and saying, "There is nothing wrong with achieving those things," and I would agree, but there is something wrong when those desires take such a foothold that you place your trust in them. There is nothing wrong about enjoying the fruits of our labor. In fact, the Lord encourages this in a way that is honoring to Him. It is when you replace the word "God" with "Me" that the ship takes a different direction.

Let's be honest with each other for a second. Ask yourself the following question:

What do you place your trust in?

Do you place it in yourself? Meaning, look at what I have created. Look at how intelligent and gifted I am at what I do, and therefore I am in control. Do you place it in status? Do you place it in your job? Do you place it in money? Do you place it in drugs or alcohol? Trust is always being placed somewhere, and the question is only "where"! Only you can answer that question honestly.

I will tell you where I place my trust, and maybe this will shock you. Ready . . . me. That's right—I place it in me, and I am not proud of it. The bottom line is that it is not easy to make it not about me in the world we live in. We are constantly told through commercials and ads that hit us on TV, cell phones, Internet, email, and billboard signs that we need something we're missing. The media is in constant demand for our money, but even deeper, it wants our hearts' desires. It wants us to wrap the meaning of our lives around buying what it is selling. The reality is that neither personal success nor material possessions that anyone has to offer can ever reveal the true meaning of life. These items may fill a sensational void, but it will be only for a moment before they slip away, only to be replaced with some other objects. How can you build your trust in something that will eventually break or get old?

So we fix our eyes not on what is seen, but on what is unseen.
For what is seen is temporary, but what is unseen is eternal.
2 Corinthians 4:18 NKJV

We run around in a constant search to fill this void. In this running around, we seek to gain some level of control. Why is it that I think I have so much control over my life? Recently, my brother-in-law told me the principal at the school where he works was killed by someone running a red light. The principal was 37 and left a wife and two daughters. That could have been me. That could have been you. So I want to ask you again, what do you place your trust in? You place it somewhere. Is it in your bank account? Your résumé? Your house? What is it? Maybe you say you place it with God, which is great. Then answer the following: How well do you do it? Where can you improve? How can you help others to trust Him?

What I do know is where I should place my trust, but like all of us, I fail on a daily basis. Simply, we live in a fallen world of lies that wants to entrap us in its web of false promises. Go buy a new car, and I promise they will come out with a better model in a couple of years. Buy the dream home, and the toilet will break and the roof will leak someday. Go get the new iPhone, and be rest assured a better one is already on the drawing board. There is only one thing that has been consistent and will never get old nor lose its luster. There is only one truth, and it comes from the One who laid down His life for you and me. The one who carried all of your sins to a cross, so that you may live in eternity with your Creator. It is our heavenly Father Jesus Christ who died on Calvary.

Please know I am not a pastor, missionary, or a person you will find preaching on the street corner. I am just a man whose heart's desire is to be more like Jesus and who knows that as a born-again Christian I want to trust Him in all that I do. It is the reason that I have made this rule a chapter in this book. Again, maybe you are reading this and it upsets you that I am writing about this in a financial book. It is not my intention to upset you, but the Lord placed it on my heart, and I needed to share where I ultimately seek my advice.

What encouragement for us all to know that we are truly not alone and we are loved by our Creator. The following verse can be found in the Holy Bible:

"Trust in the Lord with your heart, and lean not on your own understanding; in all your ways acknowledge Him, and He shall direct your paths."
Proverbs 3:5-6 NKJV

I love the way it starts: "Trust in the Lord." What is trust? It is putting your faith in the hands of someone else with the idea that they will protect you. God is saying, to us, if you trust me and remove yourself and you allow me to work in your life, then I will guide you along a path, which will bring you the wisdom to see so that your feet are established in my ways.

This verse is describing the Lord's desire for our lives and how much He cares about our future, and yet we fail to see that His path is greater and more prosperous than ours. Somehow, through our technological advances and medical breakthroughs, we can forget where we have come from.

As I finish this book, I live in a great country, the United States of America, that is a part of a world struggling in rough economic times. Unemployment is high, countries cannot pay their bills, and the road ahead seems long and uncertain for many. This is why I placed this rule in the book, and it is THE RULE to break, for our trust is found in God. I would like to leave you with one of my favorite verses in the Bible:

"I love those who love me, and those who seek me diligently will find me."
Proverbs 8:17 NKJV

God's promise to you is simple. Trust Him as your savior and pursue a personal relationship with Him, and your path will become His path.

It is my hope and prayer that this book has touched your life and equipped you with knowledge to be a wiser investor, so that you can impact the world around you. And if you are reading this last chapter and you do not have a personal relationship with Christ, it would be my encouragement to seek out a local church and discover what the Lord has for your life.

May your life be rich with His blessing!